PRAISE FOR MARY MACLANE

"Anyone who reads her will **never forget her voice**." - *Biographile* "Mary MacLane comes off the page quivering with life. **Moving**." - *London Times* "She reminds us of the **power of personal narrative**, honestly told." - *The Atlantic* "In a pre-sound-bite age she already knew **how to draw blood in one direct sentence**." - *The Awl* "She had a short but fiery life of writing and misadventure, and her writing was **a template for the confessional memoirs that have become ubiquitous**." - *The New Yorker* "One of the **most fascinatingly self-involved personalities of the 20th century**." - *The Age* "Confessional journalists have **people like Mary Mac-Lane** to thank." - *Flavorwire* "Her diaries ignited a **national uproar**, ushering in a **new era** for women's voices. Her elegant, ambitious embrace of **full-disclosure opened a door to what was possible for women**." - *The Atlantic* "**Fiery frankness** made her a pioneer." - *Time Out Chicago* "Her poetry is one of extremes: **lust for happiness, despair for life**." - *Hairy Dog Review* "Riveting." - New Hampshire Public Radio "*I Await the Devil's Coming* is a small **masterpiece, full of camp and swagger**." - Parul Sehgal, NPR "First of the self-expressionists, and **the first of the Flappers**." - *Chicagoan* "This book is the **heart cry** of **youth not yet at home** in the world. Where, since Emily Brontë, can we find this **lightning-like intuition**, and this special kind of **simple, vivid, flashing** English - **direct, rhythmic, beautiful**?" - Harriet Monroe "Little short of **a miracle**. No more **marvelous book** was ever born out of a **sensitive, precocious** brain." - Clarence Darrow "She senses the **infinite resilience**, the **drunken exuberance**, the **magnificent power and delicacy of the language**." - H.L. Mencken

*

OUR PAST MACLANE BOOKS

"A **girl wonder**." - *Harper's* (two-page exclusive spread) "A **pioneering feminist - a sensation**." - *Feminist Bookstore News* "From now on *Tender Darkness* must take **a prominent place in any discussions of American women's writing** and the **literature of the West**." - Dr Peter Donahue, Oklahoma State University - "A **pioneering newswoman** and later a **silent-screen star**, considered **the veritable spirit of the iconoclastic Twenties**, 'the **Joan of Arc** of the Red-Hot Mamas.' 'How did it happen,' declared one of her eulogists, 'that **a revolution in manners started, or seemed to start, with an unruly young woman** who couldn't bear the sight of the toothbrushes hanging up in the family bathroom at **Butte, Montana**?'" - Robert Taylor, Chief Critic, *Boston Globe*

*

Michael R. Brown is the foremost Mary MacLane researcher in the world today. He authored the well-reviewed experimental memoir *She and I: A Fugue* and in 2014 completed the 600-page anthology *Human Days: A Mary MacLane Reader*. He is completing a multi-volume series on MacLane's life, career, and influence for publication in 2015. He lives in Northern California.

By the Editor:

She and I: A Fugue

Human Days: A Mary MacLane Reader

I Await the Devil's Coming: Annotated & Unexpurgated

Tender Darkness: A Mary MacLane Sampler

http://fuguewriter.com

*

Coming in 2015:

*Mary in The Press:
Miss MacLane and Her Fame*

*A Quite Unusual Intensity of Life:
The Lives, Works and Influence of
Mary MacLane*

(with Chiara di Benedetto)

I, MARY MACLANE

A Diary of Human Days

EDITED, WITH A FOREWORD &
NOTES, BY MICHAEL R. BROWN

PETRARCA PRESS
AUSTIN · TEXAS
2014

The foreword, notes, bibliography,
and all other new material are copyright
© 2014 by Petrarca Press. Permission is
granted for brief quotations therefrom
for critical and scholarly purposes.

First edition.

Printed in the USA.

This paper is PH-balanced.
It should undergo lessened crumbling,
yellowing, or other deterioration over time.

BIBLIOGRAPHIC DATA

MacLane, Mary, 1881-1929
I, Mary MacLane: a diary of human days
1st ed. / p. cm.
Includes bibliographic references (p.).
Lib. of Congress Control No. PENDING
1. Feminism - United States - Literary collections
2. Women - United States - Literary collections
ISBN 978-1-883304-09-6 - Paperbound
ISBN 978-1-883304-10-2 - Casebound

Table of Contents

Foreword

MARY MACLANE suffered and benefited from one of the most sensational debuts in literary history. *I Await the Devil's Coming* (published in 1902 as *The Story of Mary MacLane*) brought the kind of wealth, notoriety, press mobs, and hanging-on-every-word some writers dare not even dream of. That she'd written at age 19, and published at 20, intensified it all.

Her second book, *My Friend Annabel Lee* of 1903, was a deliberate feint of the public's hunger for more sexuality, brimstone, and the hard-edge. It seems written in indefinite space, between moods, about elusive matters. Conceived in a hotel by the sea, its ruling element is water as *I Await's* was fire. *Annabel*, she said, "is made up of reflections and impressions and sketches ... I take the part of a foil to my friend Annabel Lee," which she called "particularly effective contrasted with the all-egotistic part I take in the other book." (*Literary News*, Aug 1903, p 255) But the impressions' sources, and of what they are made, are often irreducibly obscure. This is no lessening of her art; on the contrary: the book works on its own, and also, as often with her, there are parallels to movements in high-art worlds: for instance, to Debussy's pushing impressional fluidity further in *La Mer*, begun in *Annabel's* publication-year.

But there was no permanent shift. Her post-*Annabel* newspaper work shows substantially the same voice and posture, if a bit looser and more playful (possibly under the influence of vaudeville), as before. The book was a stylistic mode, conditioned to a particular situation and consequent intention.

So there was no telling what her next would be like.

It wouldn't be started for almost a decade, and not finished for almost half-a-decade after that. It would be as little a continuation of *I Await* as it would be of *Annabel*. It was a turn on a new axis then a stride to a new horizon. If it was a feint, it was non-linear: by synthesizing the previous two while staying free of them, it formed her books into a trinity. Just as *Annabel* is unpredicted by *I Await*, *I Mary* cannot be predicted from the other two.

It is her longest, most-involved, and deepest book - and her last. Its writing began the final stage of her career, and publication led to her last public accomplishment: writing and starring as herself, later in 1917, in her ground-breaking silent movie - *Men Who Have Made Love to Me*.

MacLane's career, inner and outer, is yet to be interpreted in full. There is no canon of thought on her - not yet - and her texts, looked at in merited depth, have enough to keep literary analysers long-occupied. A few words, then, to place this last book in the fullness of her book-length work. (Her complete works, including the correspondence and newspaper features, will be examined in a book-length biographical study by the editor now in preparation.)

I Await is suffused with excellence in style and perceptivity, with sincerity of confession and meta-confession (*e.g.*, admissions of not-quite-honesty) - and conscious presentment of a warriorress sprinkled with droplets of part-innocent girl, the whole held up shakily against a threatful background. Here, we see between each line, is one worthy of life, worth saving and attending-to. The great enemy is Butte, and the right thing to do is buy the author's book - as she broke the fourth wall in film in 1917, she breaks it in literature in 1901 - and help her to escape. Her personal appeal could not, by the end, be more open and direct.

By 1903, she had escaped. Wealthy, famed for infamy, focus of America's newspaper eye, she'd left Butte and by October of 1902 had escaped the public voracity about her person by lodging in a shore hotel on the Atlantic coast. There she began her *Annabel*, which she'd continue as she met and moved in with an older woman who'd been life-partner to the well-known author Maria Louise Pool before her death in 1898. On a river-borne trip to Montreal in July 1903, MacLane finished the book.

Where the first book bore definite aims, often set down with searing incisiveness and hauteur, the second is in content a near-random assemblage, in mood a thorough dissolution of definite form into drifting shapes reminiscent of very late Romanticism, e.g., of Liszt in *Nuages gris* (cited as a premonitor of, again, Impressionism in music); in style, she is if anything stronger: the line of attention is less broken, the fourth wall is firmly reestablished (and may partly inform the book's closing scene), and the clarity of the writing impregnable.

She generally didn't discuss literary intentions in public, so we have no testimony on the purposes or methods behind her final book. But inspection of the three in sequence displays an intention in *I, Mary* to reveal herself as never before through a synthesis and transcendence of the prior books' approaches.

The direct focus on self - constant in *I Await*, absent in *Annabel* - returns. *Annabel's* watery flowiness is retained, while the edge of *I Await* is held to service. The stylistic attention is, if anything, intenser than before, but the grammar-underlayment of the two previous - a solid, essentially conservative, proper late-19th-century British-toned American English - has been torn out for a more modern, experimental remodel, complete with incessant coinages, an expanded vocabulary, and relentless forward motion.

But it is in subject matter that *I, Mary* walks furthest away from its predecessors, indeed from the rest of her work. She'd said that "the unhuman aloofness which once was mine" had been destroyed by her stint living in New York in 1908-1909. (*Butte Evening News*, 22 May 1910, p 9) *I, Mary* is its author's last farewell to that aloofness and all it had subserved. It would never be heard again, and she pushed self-disclosure in *I, Mary* to such extremes that it wouldn't have been credited.

In *I, Mary*, the author breaks through prior walls to give her momentary, imperfect, vulnerable, spontaneous self. No longer is there a fourth wall - neither is there a first through third. The author explicitly invites us inside herself, and to some partial merging with "the flat unglowing bloody Self Just Beneath My Skin."

The book crackles with uncanny energy. For some years the editor privately called it "Mary's Black Book" and spoke of it as almost a volume to cast spells by. The composure she maintains in all the rest of her work is gone, and for years it seemed too much. But as MacLane's career came clearer, its place emerged, and suddenly it all made heart-gripping sense: MacLane trusts us enough to show herself desperate, rapt, miserable, transported, leaden, enraged, sanguine.

The manner of her first book was not to be imposed, even as a schematic ghost. In each book a separate world is created - or, rather, a separate world-facet of the author is expressed to completion.

And so, here is the book created in Butte once again, whose ruler is this time neither fire, nor water, but that which somehow moderates between the two: blood.

Michael R. Brown
Butte County, California
November 2014

P.S. On the following page I give, for interpretive interest and to note a textual issue, the introduction to *I, Mary* in *Human Days*.

MacLane's final book was her testament in every way and concludes the evolution begun in I Await. *She had vowed to explode out into the world from Butte, and now she turns within and ranges through her internal world. Taking the static and neutral-toned* Annabel Lee *as center, her three books balance neatly.*

Written from c. 1911 to 1917, I Mary *seems both impromptu and outside of time. Superficially emulative of the dated-entry format of* I Await, *it positions the reader in the most intimate contact MacLane would ever permit: we are with her inside herself, in - except for the first and, movingly, a later entry - an eternal tomorrow. The martial author of* I Await, *who stood off and upbraided the world, is absent;* Annabel's *two personae have evidently fused in order to problematize the inner world. Here, MacLane seems to say: watch my givens as they pass; below these I will not go, and they are neither good nor evil - they simply exist. Yet her humor - dry, sly, strongest at her (as she might say) seriousest - never deserts us.*

It is not known if MacLane read Nietzsche - her iconoclastic sometime supporter H.L. Mencken was an early American advocate, and he'd read Max Stirner - but if I Await *was an exercise in self-assertion,* I, Mary *ventures into a self-criticism probably entirely uninfluenced by Freud.*

This book was issued by Gertrude Atherton's publisher, Frederick A. Stokes Co., and an editorial challenge is presented by their abandonment of left-indention throughout. Although this echoes MacLane's holograph practices (her left-indents, always narrow, disappear by 1917), it renders one unable to ascertain after a flush-right full stop or sentence-terminal dash whether a new paragraph begins or not.

Pending discovery of the MS - no trace has yet been found - the editor has inserted paragraph starts where they seem called-for on logical, rhythmic, or stylistic grounds - but retained flush-left for all dash-enclosed asides (which he gives in italics, to further set off from running text). Readers who wish to view the text as originally published will find it available on the Internet at no charge.

I, MARY MACLANE

A Diary of Human Days

- 1917 -

To
M- T-

these Live Fruits
from the Withered Garden

*

A Crucible of My Own Making

It is the edge of a somber July night in this Butte-Montana.

The sky is overcast. The nearer mountains are gray-melancholy.

And at this point I meet Me face to face.

I am Mary MacLane: of no importance to the wide bright world and dearly and damnably important to Me.

Face to face I look at Me with some hatred, with despair and with great intentness.

I put Me in a crucible of my own making and set it in the flaming trivial Inferno of my mind. And I assay thus:

I am rare - I am in some ways exquisite.

I am pagan within and without.

I am vain and shallow and false.

I am a specialized being, deeply myself.

I am of woman-sex and most things that go with that, with some other *pointes.*

I am dynamic but devasted, laid waste in spirit.

I'm like a leopard and I'm like a poet and I'm like a religieuse and I'm like an outlaw.

I have a potent weird sense of humor - a saving and a demoralizing grace.

I have brain, cerebration - not powerful but fine and of a remarkable quality.

I am scornful-tempered and I am brave.

I am slender in body and someway fragile and firm-fleshed and sweet.

I am oddly a fool and a strange complex liar and a spiritual vagabond.

I am strong, individual in my falseness: wavering, faint, fanciful in my truth.

I am eternally self-conscious but sincere in it.

I am ultra-modern, very old-fashioned: savagely incongruous.

I am young, but not very young.

I am wistful - I am infamous.

In brief, I am a human being.

I am presciently and analytically egotistic, with some arresting dead-feeling genius.

And were I not so tensely tiredly sane I would say that I am mad.

So assayed I begin to write this book of myself, to show to myself in detail the woman who is inside me. It may or it mayn't show also a type, a universal Eve-old woman. If it is so it is not my purport. I sing only the

Ego and the individual.

So does in secret each man and woman and child who breathes, but is afraid to sing it aloud. And mostly none knows it is that he does sing. But it is the only strength of each. A bishop serving truly and tirelessly the poor of his diocese serves a strong vanity and ideal of the Ego in himself. A starving sculptor who lives in and for his own dreams is an Egotist equally with the bishop. And both are Egotists equally with me.

Egotist, not egoist, is my word: it and not the idealized one is the "winged word."

It is made of glow and gleam and splendor, that Ego. I would be its votary.

So I write me this book of Me - my Soul, my Heart, my sentient Body, my magic Mind: their potentialities and contradictions.

- there is a Self in each human one which lives and has its sweet vain someway-frightful being not in depths and not in surfaces but Just Beneath The Skin. It is the Self one keeps for oneself alone. It is the Essence of soul and bones. It is the slyest subtlest thing in human scope. It is the loneliest: tragically lonely. It is long, long isolation - beautiful, terrifying, barbarous, shameful, trivial to points of madness, ever-present, infinitely intriguing to oneself, passionately hidden: hidden forever and forever -

It is my aim to write out that in the pages of this Me-book: no depths save as they come up and touch that, no surfaces save as they sink skin-deep. Only the flat unglowing bloody Self Just Beneath My Skin.

I shall fail in it, partly because my writing skill is unequal to some nice-nesses in the task, but mostly because I am not very honest even with myself.

I'll come someway near it.

*

Half Inevitably, Half by Choice

To-morrow

Half inevitably, half by choice, I write this book now.

I am at a lowering impatient shoulder-shrugging life-point where I must express myself or lose myself or break.

And I am quite alone as I live my life.

And I am unhappy - a scornful unhappiness not of bitter positive grief which admits of engulfing luxuries of sorrow, but of muffled unrests and tortures of knowing I fit in nowhere, that I drift - drift - and it brings an unbearable dread, always more and more dread, into days and into wakeful nights.

And writing it turns the brunt of it a little away from me.

And to write is the thing I most love to do.

And I myself am the most immediate potent topic I can find in my knowledge to write on: the biggest, the littlest, the broadest, the narrowest, the loveliest, the hatefulest, the most colorful, the most drab, the most mystic, the most obvious, and the one that takes me farthest as a writer and as a person.

I write myself when I write the thoughts smouldering in me whether they be of Death, of Roses, of Christ's Mother, of Ten-penny Nails.

One's thoughts are one's most crucial adventures. Seriously and strongly and intently to contemplate doing murder is everyway more exciting, more romantic, more profoundly tragic than the murder done.

I unfold myself in accursed and precious written thoughts. I cast the reflections of my inner selves on the paper from the insolent mirror of my Mind.

- my Mind - it is so free -

My Soul is not free: God hung a string of curses, like a little manacling chain, round its neck long and long ago. Always I feel it. My Heart is not free for it is dead: in a listless way and a trivial way, dead. And my Body - it is free but has a seeming of something wasted and useless like a dinner spread out on a table uneaten and growing cold.

- but my free Mind -

Though I were shut fast in a prison: though I were strapped in an electric chair: though I were gnawed and decayed by leprosy: I still could *think*, with thoughts free as gold-drenched outer air, thoughts delicate-luminous as young dawn, thoughts facile, seductive, speculative, artful, evil, sly, sublime.

You might cut off my two hands: but you could not keep me from remembering the Sad Gray Loveliness of the Sea when the Rain beats, beats, beats upon it.

You might admonish me by driving a red-hot spike between my two white shoulders: but you could not by that influence my Thoughts - you could not so much as change their current.

I am intently aware of my Mind from moment to moment - all the passing life-moments. The awareness is a troubled power, a heavy burden and a wild enchantment. -

Also what I feel I write.

I am my own law, my own oracle, my own one intimate friend, my own guide though I guide me to dead-walls, my own mentor, my own foe, my own lover.

I am in age one-and-thirty, a smouldering-flamed period which feels the wings of the Youth-bird beating strong and violent for flight - half-ready to fly away.

I am not a charming person. Quite seventy singly-used adjectives would better fit me.

But I have some charm of youth, and a charm of sex, and a charm of intellect and intuition, and some charms of personality.

I have a perfervid appreciation of those things in other persons. And my steel has sometime struck fire from their flint.

But always my steel has turned back drearily yet strongly to itself.

*

A Twisted Moral

To-morrow

If I should meet God to know and speak to the first thing but one I should ask him would be, "What was your idea, God, in making me?"

I can believe he had some Purpose in it.

I'm in most ways a devilish person. There's sevenfold more evil than good in me. It is evil of a mixed and menacing kind, the kind that goes dressed in brave and beauty-tinted clothes and is sane and sound. While the good in me is ill and forlorn and nervously afraid - a something of tear-blurred eyes and trembling fingers.

Yet God has made many things less plausible than me. He has made sharks in the ocean, and people who hire children to work in their mills and mines, and poison ivy, and zebras -

- and he has made besides a Wonder of things: Thin Pink Mountain Dawns, Young English Poets, Hydrangeas in the sudden Blue of their first Bloom, human Singing Voices, - more things, always more -

When I think of them all a joyous thrill breaks over me like a little frenzied wave. It is delirium-of-bliss to feel oneself living though shadows be pitch-black.

God has a Purpose in making everything, I think.

I am half-curious about the Purpose that goes with me. He might have made me for his own amusement. He might have made me to discipline my Soul with some blights and goads or to punish it for bacchanalian ease and pleasure in the long-distant centuries-old past. He might have made me to season or scourge other lives, as I may touch them, with Mary-Mac-Lane-ness. He might have made me to point a twisted moral.

I muse about it with doubts.

But if I knew my Purpose I belike would not swerve a hair's-breadth from my own course which is an unhallowedly selfish one.

If I could myself see a way of truth I would walk in it. I have it in me to worship. I long to worship. And I am game, wearily and coldly game: when I start I go on through to the end.

But I see no way of truth - none for me. And God is eternally absent and reticent. So I go on in the way where I find myself. And muse about it. And damn it faintly as I make nothing of it.

*

Everyday and To-morrow

To-morrow

Aloofly I live in this Butte in the outward rôle of a family daughter with no responsibilities.

This Butte is an incongruous living place for me.

And I have not one human friend in it - no kindliness. And Nature in her perplexingest mood would not of herself have cast me as a family daughter. Three things have kept me thus for four years past: that nothing has called me out of it: a slight family pressure like a tiny needle-point which pierces only if one moves: and to stay thus is presently the line of least resistance.

Unless impelled to violent action by a violent reason - like love or hatred or jealousy or a baby or humiliated pride or rowelling ambition - a woman follows the physical line of least resistance. I have followed it these years with outward acquiescence and inward rages - languid rages which lay me waste.

The years and acquiescences and rages have built up a mood which compasses me, drives me, damns me, and lifts me up.

It is a forceful mood, though I am not myself forceful.

This mood is this book. -

I live an immoral life. It is immoral because it is deadly futile. All my Tissues of body, soul, mind, and heart are wasting, decaying, wearing down, minute by minute, hour by hour, day by day: with no return to me or to my life, nor to anything human or divine.

It makes me dread my life and myself.

I do not quite know why.

But to be an ardent pickpocket or an eager harlot would feel honester.

My Everyday goes like this: I waken in the morning and lie listless some minutes with drooping eyelids. I look at a gilt-and-blue bar of morning light which slants palely in at one window and at a melting-gold triangle of sun which shows at the other window on the red brick wall of the house next to this. Then I say "another day," and I kick off bed-covers with one foot and slide out of my narrow bed, and into blue slippers, and out of a thin nightgown, and into peignoir or bathrobe. I twist and flatten and gather up my tangled hair and push some amber pins through it. And I go into a respectable green-and-gray bathroom and draw a bath and get into it. I splash in brief swift soapsuds, and go under a sudden heroic icy cold shower, and dry me with a scourging towel. Then I go back into the blue-white bed-room and get into clothes, feminine thin under-garments and a nunlike frock.

I look in my mirror. Some days I'm a delicately beautiful girl. Other days I'm a very plain woman.

One's physical attractiveness is a matter of one's mental chemistry.

I say to Me in the mirror, "It's you-and-me, Mary MacLane, and another wasting damning To-morrow.

To-morrow and to-morrow and to-morrow
Creeps in this petty pace from day to day."

A haunting decadence is in that To-morrow thought. And always the To-morrow thought comes out of my morning mirror.

I dwell on it awhile, till my gray eyes and my lips and my teeth and my forehead are tired of it, and make nothing new of it.

I jerk the flat scollop of hair at one side of my forehead and turn away. I open door and windows wider for the blowing-through of breezes. And I wander down-stairs. It is half-after nine or half-after ten. I go into the clean empty clock-ticking kitchen and cook my breakfast. It is a task full of hungry plaisance and pleasantness. I make a British-feeling breakfast of tea and marmalade and little squares of toast and pink-and-tan rashers of bacon and two delightful eggs. Up to the moment of broaching the eggs the morning has an ancient sameness with other mornings. But eggs, though I've eaten them every day for quite five-and-twenty years, are always a fascinating novelty.

They are delicious in my breakfast. So are the squares of toast and the bacon-rashers and the tea and marmalade. When I've done with them I lay down my napkin by my cup, light a cigarette, breathe a puff or two from it and feel contentedly aware that my brain has gone to rest in sweet tranquility with my breakfast. When my brain is in my head it analyzes the soul out of my body, the gleam out of my gray eyes, the savor out of my life, the human taste off my tongue. That post-breakfast moment is the only peace-moment I know in my day and in my life.

Having puffed away the cigarette and read bits of a morning paper I then prove me arrantly middle-class by contemplating washing my breakfast dishes.

I am middle-class, quite, from the Soul outward. But it is not specially apparent - one's tastes and aspirations flit garbledly far and wide. But a tendency to wash one's dishes after eating one's breakfast feels conclusively and pleasantly middle-class. Not that I do always wash them, but always I think of it with the inclination to do it.

I sit on the shaded front veranda in the summer noon day and look away south at the blue Highlands, ever snow-peaked: or east at the near towering splendid grim wall of the arid Rockies which separates this Butte from New York, from London, - the Spain-castles - the Pyramids - the Isle of Lesbos: or south-west beyond house-tops at some foothills above which hangs a fairy veil made by melting together a Lump of Gold and an Apricot and spreading it thin.

Then restlessly I go into the house and up to my room. I put it in order - in prim, prim immaculate order. One marked phase of mine is of some wanton creature - a mænad, a mental Amazon, a she-imp. But playing opposite to that is another - that of a New-England spinster steel-riveted to certain neat ferociously-orderly habits. A stray thread on my blue rug hurts, *hurts* me until I pick it up. Dust around my room gives me a nervous pain, a piteous gnawing grief-of-the-senses, until I've removed it. And my chastened-looking bed - after I've turned over its tufted mattress and "made" it, smooth and white and crisp and soft - how the fibers of me would writhe should anyone sit on it. But no one sits on it. And I myself sooner than press one finger-tip down into its perfectness would sell my body to a Balkan soldier for four dimes: it is that way I feel about it. My bed *must* be kept perfect till the moment I slip into it at night to float under the dream-worlds.

Then maybe I pull a soft black hat down over my hair and draw on gloves and go out into the gray-paved streets for a longish walk. Or maybe the day is humidly hot. Then I don't go but stay in the blue-white room and mend a bit of torn lingerie or a handkerchief or a silk stocking or a petticoat. Or I take books and dig out some Greek - Homer or a Sapphic fragment - very laboriously but marveling that I can do it at all: the first thing one forgets being the last things one learned at school. Or I read an English or a French philosopher, or a translated Tolstoy, or a bit of Balzac novel, or some bits of Dickens-books with which latter I am long familiar and long enamored for the restful falseness of their sentiment and the pungent appetizing charm of their villains.

And betweenwhiles I think and think.

Then it's dinnertime and I perhaps change into the other nunlike dress, and nibble some dinner with no appetite, and talk with the assembled small family in a vein and tone of life-long insincerity. When in family-circle-ness I've had to hide my true self as if behind a hundred black veils since the age of two years. It would be a poignant effort now to show any of it at the family dinners, which is the only meeting-time. The one easy way is to be comprehensively insincere at the dinners where with no appetite I nibble. None there wants my sincerity, and so in my Soul's accounting now it is eternally and determinedly No Matter. It is a little bell which stopped ringing long and long ago. If it rang now it would ring only No-Matter, No-Matter.

Then it's night and I go to take the walk I didn't take in the afternoon. I walk down long lonely streets. Long lonely thoughts pile into me and through me and wrap me in a nebula that I can feel around me like a mantle. I walk two or three miles of paved streets till I'm very tired. I am lithe but fragile from constant involuntary self-analysis. One may analyze one's life-experience and life-emotion till physical tissues at times grow frail, gossamer-thin. It is then as if - at a word, a whispered thought, a beat of the heart - one's Soul might flutter through the Veil, join light hands with the death-angel, and flee away.

- but I love my life even while I analyze it bit by bit and so hate it. I love it in its grating monotones and its moments of glow and its days of shadow and storm and bitterish lowering passion -

I walk back beneath a night sky of dusky velvet-blue decked with jewels of moon and star and flying bright-edged cloud. The night has a subdued preciousness, like an illicitly pregnant woman's. It is big with the bastard-exquisite To-morrow. The night air kisses my lips and throat. I pull off my gloves to feel it on my hands. It gives me a charmed and unexciting feeling of being caressed without being loved.

I come back to my blue-white room, take off my hat, ruffle my fingers through my hair, look at Me in the mirror and smile the melancholy wicked smile which I keep for Me-alone. It's an intimate moment of greeting - a recognition of my Familiar on coming back to her. Often when I walk I go without Me, and wander far from Me, and forget Me.

Then I sit at my flat black desk and write desultorily for two or three or four hours. Sometimes a letter, sometimes some verses or a hectic fancy in staid prose. But now mostly this.

Then I go downstairs to a refrigerator or a cellar-way to find food - a slice off an affable cold joint, some chaste-looking slices of bread, a slim innocent onion. And I eat them, not relishingly but voraciously, reminding myself of a lean foraging furtive coyote. It is two or three or four in the morning. I smoke a quiet cigarette in a cool night doorway and count the nervous gray-velvet moths outside the screen.

And all the while I think and think.

Then I come up to my room and sit on the floor by my low bookcase and read some last-century English poets - the Brownings and Shelley and the unspeakable John Keats. The Poets make me a space of incalescent magic and loveliness. They are the beings blest of a flaming Heaven. In the midst of soddenest earthiness their fiery wings "pierce the night."

Then I'm thrilledly tired. I close the books and make ready for my bed in a lyric-feeling languor. A soft soothing unsnapping of whalebone stays: a muffled rhythmic undoing of metal-and-silk-rubber garters: a pushing down and sliding out of daytime clothes and into a thin pale cool silk nightgown: a hurried brushing of hair: an anointing of hands and throat with faint-scented cream: a goodnight to Me in the mirror: a last wave of a fateful thing - my life-essence - casual and determined and contemptuous and menacing - sweeping down over me in an invisible shower: and I'm betwixt smooth linen sheets.

In twenty seconds blest, blest sleep.

Of such wide littleness is my day made. One day will differ from another in this or that volcanic mole-hill. And some days I not only wash a great many dishes but do a deal of housework neatly and self-satisfactorily and like a devilish scullery maid.

And some days as I move in the petty pace thoughts and feelings sweet or barbarous come and change my world's face in a moment.

Also a casual human being of rabbitish brain and chipmunkish sensibility may stray across my path and gently bore me and accentuate my own paganness.

But always the same days in restless dubious To-morrowness.

Always immorally futile.

And eerily alone.

A Mathematic Dead-Wall

To-morrow

I'm put to it to decide whether God loves me or hates me when he sets me down alone.

There are times when my Loneliness is a charmed and scintillant and resourceful Loneliness with a strange and ecstatic gleam in it. The miracle of being a person rushes upon and about and into me "with lightning and with music."

One loses that in a day of many friendships.

But oftener are times when the tired, tired heart and the weary, weary brain beat-beat, beat-beat to anguished torturing self-rhythms. The spirit of me closes its eyes in turbulent dusks of wondering and wishing and leans its forehead against a mathematic dead-wall. And it prays - blind useless unhumble prayers which leave it dry and destitute, arid, unspeakably lacking. But when it lifts its head and opens its eyes there are the melting mauves and maroons of a dead sun across the evening sky, and the small far wistful flames of always-hopeful stars.

- they make it matter less whether God loves or hates me, but still I wish I knew.

*

My Neat Blue Chair

To-morrow

I suppose there's nothing quite peculiar to even my inmost self in what I ponder and what I experience and what I feel.

My only elemental "differentness" is that I find it and write it.

But I used to think at eighteen - those thrice-fired adolescent moments - that only I suffered, only I reached achingly out into the mists, only I tasted new-bloomed life-petals intolerably sweet and bitter on my lips.

The egotism of youth is merciless, measureless, endlessly vulnerable. Youth plays on itself as one plays on a little dulcimer, with music as sweet, but with a crude cruel recklessness which jerks and breaks the strings.

I have got by that stage of egotism. But I've entered on another wilder, more lawless - farther-seeing if less be-visioned.

While I sit here this midnight in a Neat Blue Chair in this Butte-Montana for what I know a legion-women of my psychic breed may be sitting lonely in neat red or neat gray or neat any-colored chairs - in Wichita-Kansas and South Bend-Indiana and Red Wing-Minnesota and Portland-Maine and Rochester-New York and Waco-Texas and La Crosse-Wisconsin and Bowling Green-Kentucky: each feeling Herself set in a wrong niche, caught in a tangle of little vapidish cross-purpose: each waiting, waiting always - waiting all her life - not hopeful and passionate like Eighteen but patient or blasphemous or scornful or volcanic like Early-Thirty: the waiting-sense giving to each a personal quality big and suggestive and nurturing - and with it a long-accustomed feeling like a thin bright blade stuck deep in her breast: each more or less roundly hating Waco-Texas and Portland-Maine and Red Wing-Minnesota and the other places: and each beset by hot unquiet humannesses inside her and an old yearn of sex and the blood warring with myriad minute tenets dating from civilization's dawn-times.

But though I am of that psychic breed no little tenets war in me.

It's as if a prelate and a wood-nymph had fathered and mothered me: making me of a ridiculous poignant conscience and of no human traditions.

I am free of innate conventionalities, free as a wildcat on a twilight hill. I am free of them as I sit here, quiet-looking, in my plain black dress. The virile Scotch-Canadian curl is brushed and brushed out of my hair to make it lie smooth and discreet over my ears and forehead. My feet are shod daintily like a charming girl's. My nails are pinkly polishedly pointed. My narrow black eyebrows look nearly patrician in their sereneness. My lips are stilly sad. My eyelids droop like the sucking dove's. But my gray eyes beneath the lids - when I raise them to the glass, my own Essence looks out of them, tiredly vivid. It seems made of languor and barbaricness and despair: and vague guiltiness, and some pure disastrous heathen religion, and lust: and lurid consciousness of everyday things and smouldering melancholy and blazing loving hatred of life.

My gray eyes out-look the wildcat's on a twilight hill.

But - so far as the Sitting goes - I sit here in my Neat Blue Chair the same as they all sit in any-colored chairs in their Wichitas and La Crosses.

*

A Lost Person

To-morrow

I am wandering about, a Lost Person, wandering and lost.

Not magnificently lost in wide Gothic forest closes, with strong great blackish green trunks and branches all around overwhelming and thrilling me.

Not dramatically lost on desert reefs with breakers riding up like menacing hosts and joyously drowning me.

But lost surprisingly in a small clump of shoulder-high hazel-brush. In it are some wood-ticks, and a few caterpillars, and a few wan spiders which spin little desultory webs from twig to twig and then abandon them for other twigs. Underfoot are unexpected wet places at intervals that my high hard heels sink into exasperatingly.

I walk round and round and across in the hazel-brush groping and knowing I'm lost in it but knowing little else of it: knowing no way out of it.

The bushes bear green leaves - rather small ones and warped because the clump is in a half-shaded place back of a hill. And they bear hazel-nuts, but not very good ones - mostly shell.

*

A Thin Damnedness

To-morrow

I own two plain black Dresses and none besides.

And I need no more.

In which two sentences I touch the crux and the keynote and the thin damnedness of my life as it is set: of my life, not of myself, for myself lives naked inside the circle of my life.

But my outer life is spaced by my Two plain Dresses. My Two Dresses measure how far removed I presently am from the wide world of things.

In the world of things a woman is judged not specifically by her morals: not invariably by her reputation: not absolutely by her money: not indubitably by her social prestige: only relatively by her beauty: and as to her brain or lack of it - la-la-la! She is judged in the matter-world simply, completely, entirely by her clothes. It is tacitly so agreed and decreed all over the earth - wherever women are of the female sex and men pursue them.

It is no injustice to any woman. It is the fairest fiat in the unwritten code.

Only a few women, the few specialized breeds, can express the fire or the humanness in them by play-acting or suffragetting or singing or painting or writing or trained-nursing or house-keeping. But there's not one - from a wandering Romany gypsy, red-blooded and strong-hearted, to an over-guarded over-bred British princess - who doesn't express what she is in the clothes she wears and the way she wears them.

Her clothes conceal and reveal, artfully and contradictorily and endlessly.

It is all a limitless field.

No actor could act Hamlet without that perfect Hamletesque black costume.

A nun's staid beautiful habit interprets her own meanings within and without.

A woman naked may look markedly pure: the same woman clothed conventionally and demurely may achieve a meanly ghoulishly foul seeming.

One either is made or marred by one's habiliments.

A woman by her raiment's make and manner can express more of her wit, her ego, her temper, her humor, her plastic pulsating personality than she could by throwing a bomb, by making a good or bad pudding, by losing her chastity, or by traducing her neighbor. The germ and shadow and likelihood of each of those acts is in the fashion and line and detail of her garments.

A jury thinks it tries a woman for a crime. Some of the twelve good and true may admit each to himself that they are trying the color of her eyes or the shape of her chin or the droop of her shoulders. But it's only her clothes they unwittingly try for murder or theft or forgery, or whatever has tripped her. It may be an alluringly shabby little dress that saves her from the gallows. It may be a hat worn at the wrong angle that is found guilty and sentenced to death. A glove in her lap, a fluttering veil, a little white handkerchief dropped to the floor by her chair - those are what the court tries for life or liberty. -

But it is I I tell about, I and my Two plain Dresses.

In me a smart frock or an unbecoming one makes a surprising difference. I impress my costume with my mixed temperament and it retaliates in kind.

One day I looked a beautiful young creature - one August Saturday in New York it was - in a tailored gown of embroidered linen. With it I wore such a good hat: its color was pale olive: its texture was soft Milan straw: its price was forty dollars. My shoes were gray silk. I so fancied myself that day that I feared lest my writing talent had gone away from me. For God takes away the beer if he gives you the skittles. And in ill-conditioned clothes - some days the weather, the devil, the soddenness of life get into one's garments and make even fair ones look ill-conditioned - I am plain-faced, plain all over - so plain that the villainies of my nature feel doubtful and I half-think I may be a good woman.

In a life full of people I would own varied delicate beautiful clothes since it is by them one is judged, and since I am quite vain. But no people are in my life. I feel deadlocked. I am caught in a vise made by my own analytic ratiocination. I am not free to live a world-life till I've someway expressed Me and learned if not whither I go at least where I stand.

So it's Two plain Dresses I own and none besides.

It may be I shall not ever again need more.

The Two Dresses are at present of serge and voile. Their identity changes with change of fashion and with wearing out. They are cut well and fit me well. But the Two does not change, nor the plainness. I change only from one Frock to the other and from the other to the one again.

I have various other clothes. A woman - whatever her traits and tempers - garners what she can of handmade under-linens and dainty nightgowns and silk hose and all such private panoply. They are the apparel of her sex rather than her individuality. The uncognizant world is unable to judge her by them. But the woman herself judges and respects herself by the goodness of her intimate garments.

My sex is to me a mystic gift. I marvel over it and clothe it silkenly.

Also I own a healthful-looking percale house-gown or two in which I do housework.

But my passing life, my eerie lonely life, is lived in my Two Dresses and none besides, and I need no more.

*

A Prison of Self

To-morrow

My Two Dresses tell me the scope of my present Mary-Mac-Lane-ness.

Every day they tell me things about myself.

They tell me I'm living in a prison of self, invisible and ascetic and somberly just.

They tell me I'm living an outer life narrow and broodingly companionless and that if I were not self-reliant by long habit a leprous morbidness would rot me in body and spirit.

They tell me because of outer solitude an inner fever of emotion and egotism and a fervid analytic light are on all my phases of self: mental, physical, psychical, and sexual.

They tell me my way of thought is at once meditative and cave-womanish.

They tell me I'm all ways the Unmarried Woman and profoundly loverless.

They tell me I'm like a child and like a sequestered savage.

They tell me I am having no restful unrealities of social life with chattering women and no monotonous casually bloodthirsty flirtations with men.

They tell me I walk daily to the edges of myself and stare into horrible-sweet egotistic abysses.

They tell me I'm grave-eyed and coldly melancholy.

They tell me there's a bereftness in the curves of my breasts and an unfulfillment in my loose-girt loins.

They tell me I am barren of sensation and fertile in feeling.

They tell me God has taken away the beer and also the skittles and left me only pieces of bread and drinks of water.

*

A Winding Sheet

To-morrow

The least important thing in my life is its tangibleness.

The only things that matter lastingly are the things that happen inside me.

If I do a cruel act and feel no cruelty in my Soul it is nothing. If I feel cruelty in my Soul though I do no cruel act I'm guilty of a sort of butchery and my spirit-hands are bloody with it.

The adventures of my spirit are realer than the outer things that befall me.

To dwell on the self that is known only to me - the self that is intricate and versatile, tinted, demi-tinted, deep-dyed, luminous, gives me an intimate delectation, a mental inflorescence, and sometimes an exaltation. It is not always so but it can be so.

But always to look back on the mass of outer events that have made my tangible life darkens my day.

Introspection throws a witching spell around me, though it may be a black one.

But retrospection wraps me in a Winding Sheet.

When the day is already dark from low-hanging clouds - and often when the sun is bright, bright, bright - I walk my floor and think of my scattered life-flotsam with a frown at the eyebrows: a coarse and heavy and twisted frown.

To-day was a leaden day. The air held a quality like the infernal breath of dead people. I leaned elbows on my dull window-sill and looked off at green and purple mountains. I tried to think of some reason - some reason tangible or poetic - for living.

I wore my brocade Chinese coat fastened down the left side with round flashing glass buttons and embroidered with blue bats and gardenias: and with it a crinkly crêpe-silk petticoat: and silk shoes and respectable white silk stockings. I felt righteous because in the forenoon I had done much housework. I worked thoroughly and well, swearing and repeating poetry softly to lend me impetus. And afterward I felt useful and good.

But having changed from Dutch cap and apron and domesticness to

I, MARY MACLANE - 27

scented silk and my sad window I grew suddenly frail and vulnerable. Shadows stormed my wall and scaled it and entered in and sacked my castle. I lounged away from my window, folded my arms in my loose blue sleeves, and slowly walked my floor. I had no strength within to combat shadows.

I picked up two alien shreds, of lint and paper respectively, from the rug, but inside me undigested and indigestible memories had their own way.

They brought close an unsatisfying and dissatisfying vista of Mary MacLanes.

There was a stubborn baby in Winnipeg-Canada, as I've heard, a baby with a white skin, coldly pensive dark-blue eyes, no hair, no voice, hand-worked muslin frocks, and a fat lumpish mien.

It was this Mary MacLane.

There was a three-year-old child, as I dimly remember, still in Canada and still stubborn, with a stout keg-like pink-and-white body, baffling blue eyes, a tiny voice, thick sun-colored curls, cambric frocks, and short white socks and a morose temper. She had one love, a yellow tortoise-shell kitten which she hugged and hugged with violence until one day it died surprisingly in her arms.

It was this Mary MacLane.

There was a seven-year-old child in Minnesota, as I well remember, still stubborn and still often morose, with a thin bony little body, conscious gray eyes, a tanned face, weather-beaten hands, untidy frocks, beautiful fluffy golden hair, a tendency to secretiveness and lies, a speculative mind, fantastic day-dreams, and a free hoydenish way of life. She had playmates but no loves except an objective love for quiet greenwoods and sweet meadows and windy hills and hay-filled barns, and for the surface details of life. She had subjective hatreds for being fussed over, for being teased, and for relatives.

It was this Mary MacLane.

There was a thirteen-year-old person, as I well remember, in a windy Montana town, who was neither girl, child, nor savage but was a mixture of the three. She had a devilish contrary will and temper, the unenlightened inexpressive wholly unattractive face and features of early adolescence, a self-love that had not the dignity of egotism, and a devouring appetite for reading. She read everything she happened on - from Voltaire to Nick Carter: from *Lady Audley's Secret* to Fox's Book of Martyrs. She read Alexander Pope and Victor Hugo and John Stuart Mill. She read *Lena Rivers* by Mary J. Holmes: also Confucius: and the Brothers Grimm. She had a long-legged lanky frame, conscious gray eyes, lovely coppery-gold dark hair, and a silly headful of tangled irrational thoughts. She had pathetic impossible day-dreams. She had few companions and no loves but much hatred for most things sane, sensible, and honest.

It was this Mary MacLane.

There was an eighteen-year-old girl in this Butte, as I well remember, with the outward savagery tamed out of her by studiousness. She was slim but no longer lanky and owned a white-hot aliveness and a grace. She had repelling gray eyes and the beautiful coppery hair, and about her an isolation, a complete aloofness. Her spirit fed itself on wonderful and exquisite dreams alternated by moods of young passionate woe, analyzed and torn to shreds: all of it hid beneath a very quiet surface. She had outwardly a tense markedly virginal quality but was inwardly insolently *demi-vierge*. She had no companions, no friendships. She absorbed herself in digging knowledge out of her high school text books, studying and imagining over it, and wandering in the fascinating highways which it opened to her. She was at her moment of brain-awakening, soul-awakening, sex-awakening, life-awakening, world-awakening: it uncurtained windows of magic old sorrow for her to look from. She had no characteristic weaknesses - she was strongly and scornfully courageous. It and the need of self-expression, born of her teeming spirit and life-long suppression of it, led her to write herself out in a book, which was published. It was a poetic book and had insight and vision and a riot of color with youth as its keynote. And it was human and figuratively and literally full of the devil. The far-and-wide public in England and America read it, and the newspapers made a loud noise about it, and the lonely girl who wrote it found herself oddly notorious. It brought money which made her free of Butte and it brought human things into her life which changed her life forever. And it brought her no inner or outer excitement or elation.

It was this Mary MacLane.

There was a girl of six-and-twenty in Boston and in New York who had half-forgot her long-familiar Ego for several years. She lived and moved in folly and triviality and falseness. From having had too few companions she had too many who did her no good and no harm but helped her waste passing days and dissipate her moods and mental tissues. She had grown worldly in taste, weak in manner of thought, fragile in body from a mad irregularity of food and sleep, and in every attribute uncertain of herself. Her Soul lay sleeping: her Heart because it felt too keenly worked overtime: nothing engaged her Mind. But her analytic trend stayed by and with it she pulled to bits the varied fragmentary things she encountered. She learned New York town in human sordid enlightening disciplining ways. She learned people of many kinds in many ways. She learned other young women, which depressed and exhilarated and perplexed her. She learned men - a race whose make and motive toward women bears no analysis. She had not the usual defensive armor of the normal woman, for she was not a normal woman but certain trends of varying individuals gathered into one sensitive woman-envelope. She was careless toward men in their crude sex-rapacity in ways no "regular" woman would dare or care to be. No man could wring one tear from her, nor cause a quickening of her foolish Heart, nor any emotion in her save mirth. And there were women friends - There were some friendships whose ill effects she will never recover from, from having bestowed too much of herself on them in the headlong newness of knowing and owning friendship after her long young loneliness.

- she could not cherish anything sanely. She couldn't stand in her doorway and watch a pretty bird flying above a green hedge, and admire it for the gleam of its brilliant wings in the sun, and let it go. She must needs run out - leaving her door standing open and tea-and-cakes untasted within - and follow where the bird flew, through mire and brier, round the world -

From the odd notoriety were many letters and experiences and adventures. She met some famous persons - writers, actors, artists - of agreeable philosophic plaisances. She saw her book of youth burlesqued with artistic piquance in the Weber-and-Fields show of its season (with one Collier, adroitest of comedians, cast as her long-lost Devil). There was a hasty voyage to the edge of Europe - a voyage of terrific seasickness lying in her stateroom: a half-glimpse of Paris all gray and green in the rain: a whole glimpse of London, mystic, Dickensesque, and roundly British in its yellow-brown fog: and back again within ten days with more berth-ridden seasickness lasting from Cherbourg to New York harbor: the whole adventure grown from a Spring morning impulse. There were winters in Florida at sun-flooded resort towns full of gaudiness and gambling and surprising winter-resort people. Those were mongrel wastrel years empty of every realness, every purpose, every vantage: they filled her with a bastard wisdom.

It was this Mary MacLane.

There was a girl of seven-and-twenty worn to psychic fragments and returned on a winter's day in a mood of indifference to this Butte. It was her first return since she and her book had gone forth eight years before. She celebrated it by being brought low with a baleful blood-sucking demon of illness, what is called scarlet fever. Borne upon by the mountain altitude after sea-levels and getting in the way of epidemic germs, she had no chance. A strong feverish serpent wound itself around her, consuming and destroying. There were tortured dying weeks. She had never been ill before in all her life.

This was the most crucial bodily adventure she had known. It opened a new and dreadful world. There was no passing of time in those long, long weeks, no rational thinking, no day, no night, no dark, no morning, no memory. There was pain, and utter weariness, and a feeling of being hurried to her grave. There was an air of hurry in the stillness around, as if she and Death had made a date which she would be late in keeping unless she were urged on. There was a doctor, and a crisp white starched nurse, and there were interminable bitter drugs and tall narrow glasses of monotonous milk. She was endlessly disturbed by milk and medicine, and by cold spongings and changings of feverish bed-linens, and anointings with olive oil, and takings of her temperature, and sprayings of her throat: when she wanted only to sink down, down, forever and forever to the underworld. She almost sank. But God capriciously decided he had other plans for her - insomuch as decreeing she was not to be let go then. After seven weeks she tiredly rose from her bed and took stock of herself. Her rôle then was of a horrible yellow skeleton with negative gray eyes, a wreck of tissue and vitality such as only scarlet fever can achieve, and her beautiful thick coppery hair changed to a strange short mouse-colored tangle. She was a long time recovering. The scarlet demon changed her life and its meanings and energies and outlooks more effectually than if she had been trapped by a game-at-law and gaols and courts had had their toll of her. But after months, a year and a half of months, her health came back perfect if not vigorous, and her good looks - the few she ever had, and even the humanizing incongruous curls, though changed, grew long and covered her head again in a heathen frivol. A so magnificent mystery is this blood-and-flesh. It grows up again out of its ashes. Burn all of it but one cell in the scorchingest sickness and so that bones are still whole it will renew itself from that, perfect as the sweet-bay. But this mind, less magnificent and less mysterious and more delicate and dubious, rallies only by aid of the heart beneath it and the soul beyond it. Her mind came slowly out of darkened apathy. It lived in a high-walled cloister telling its languid beads by rote. But as if it sensed the sweet aura of her renewed body it at last woke strong and cold overnight and was aware again of itself and the mourning magic of being.

It was this Mary MacLane.

And after a year or two more it is this Mary MacLane.

It is I myself.

I walk my floor in leaden retrospect-days with a feel in my throat of damned and damning unfulfillment and at my eyebrows the twisted frown.

In it is dread and anguish and worriment: in it is hideous altering breaking prepollence of death.

- if my hair, just my hair, had not come back after that red fever I'd have decided - not capriciously like God but determinedly like myself - to have died by my own hand one night. It is no brave thought and it would have been no brave deed. Though it wants a lowering courage to leave life when, despite all, one loves its very textureless color, its bodiless air: not to speak of the yellow hot deathless sunshine that can not reach one in her dark grave -

But the look and feel of my hair are the look and feel of positive life, opposed to death.

To live up to my hair would keep me brave.

But the retrospects, which I can't escape, come and wrap me in the Winding Sheet.

*

The Dover Road

To-morrow

I lay down at noonday on my green couch and I had a quaint dream. I have just awakened from it in a flush of languor and comfort. And the dream is vivid in my mind. I dreamed I was married and it was pink-and-pearl dawn in my married bed-room. And in the bed one inch away from mine was not my married husband but "another man." It was no man I can recall having seen. As I look back into the dream he seems of the nowhere, a stranger. But in the dream he was no stranger. I had crudely admitted him to my night. And I had just awakened in the pink-and-white dawn and was sitting silk-gowned and ruffle-haired in my bed, cross-legged like a tailor with my elbows on my knees and my chin on my palms, idly contemplating him. And he was lying in the other narrow bed contemplating me and smiling a little. He had nice teeth and yellowish hair. The crux of the dream was the sound "off-stage" of the approaching footsteps of monsieur-the-husband. As it always is in the psychology of dreams the insistent thing in the situation was not the footsteps, nor even that they were approaching, but the sound: the elusive threat of their sound. He would presently discover us. Nobody appeared to care: not "another man" smiling so tranquilly: not I sitting musingly over-looking him who had overnight "enjoyed me": not the husband, because he never knew it - before he could open the guilty door I awoke.

A short-cut gently headlong dream. I was at once married, mixed adulterantly with an imperfect stranger, and awaiting in pleasant mild anticipation, to match the pink-and-pearl of the summer dawn, the climax in the approaching sound of my husband's footsteps. It was humorous and artistic. Unseemly preliminaries were done away with in that dream. I was given at once the one exciting worthwhile moment in it.

Having no data as to what were my husband's temper and tenor, what he looked like or who he was, I could not in the dream or out of it surmise what he would say or how he would act when he opened the door.

- a theme for idling speculation in a summer's day -

Also I wonder whence came that dream: so Unexpected: so Irrelevant to any thought in me: so Artistically Right: so Disgusting: so Dramatic: so quaintly Vulgar.

A question: to which the one answer is that unanswerable answer to all questions, propounded by Mr. F.'s Aunt - "There's milestones on the Dover road."

*

The Harp of Worn Strings

To-morrow

May I own no unleavened egotism.

May I own no egotism that is not sensitive and poignant and vibrant: a harp of Worn Strings.

The surprising world is full of non-analytic persons of ox-eyed vision and hen-headed mental calibre whose egotism is a stupendous impregnable armor: those who burned the Maid of Orleans: those who crucified the prophet of Nazareth: those who killed John Keats.

They inherit the earth, which is a Golden-Green earth, but never look at it.

They accept this life, which is Intoxicating life, but never feel its texture with their fingers.

They gather a Blue iris by a marsh-edge and let it die in their sweating hands, or let it fall to the ground as they walk, or throw it away when the Blue petals droop: without looking at it and breathing it and knowing it: without sensing the tremulous Blue to be lovelier in its wilting.

Theirs is the thick fat solidly-fierce egotism of an emperor or an infant whose main metaphysic concept is that *he* is alive, and will remain alive, and must be alive, though all around him bleed drop by drop to their death.

I have analyzed mine, and it is not so with me.

If I say I am enchanting or false or despicable it is because I know it's true. Not because I say it but because I have tested and proved it. I feel the textures of my life with the tips of my fingers. I turn my senses outward and let the old winds blow over them - icy, balmy, harsh, gentle, scorching, cooling. I suffer for it but I know those winds: songs of seas and stars and of little pebbles are in their thunderous-dim wailing: life is in the soft stinging perfume of their wings.

No breath of poetry and beauty comes to me that I do not pay for with the beating ache of my Heart, the nervous tensions of my Body, the fraying and shredding of my Soul. If any beauty or poet-thing comes easily and gives me pleasure and not pain, I know I have not yet got it and that it will come again.

It will come again: with the pain.

I can't eat cake and have it.

I can't make silk purses out of sows' ears.

Those things I learn nearly perfectly from playing on my harp with the Worn Strings.

*

A Strongly-Windy Saturday

To-morrow

It is a strongly-windy Saturday.

A thought achieves itself in my roiled-and-placid brain: that one half of me is Mad, but the other half is doubly Sane and someway over-Sane, so that in it all I break a little better than even.

*

A Someway Separate Individual

To-morrow

This body I live in is familiar and mysterious.

It is like a book of poetry to read and read again.

It has the owned sentientness of bone-and-flesh, and with it tremors fine as spirit-emotions.

My Body is more chaste than my Mind, my Heart, and my Soul. My Body if fragile is healthful, and is one with the woman-race. It moves with the sunlit cosmos. My Mind wanders in sex-chaos and muses on piquant impure things, enchanting villainies, odd inversions, whatnot. My Soul - a sweet and an exquisite Thing - its tired wings have borne it languidly down the dim stairways of many centuries, some leading in wilful perverted ways. And my Heart is a pagan Heart. Its essence is flavored with the day and lyric trail of the Sapphic students.

Bodily I am also pagan in the freedom of my owned sex feelings - as are all women. Most of them do not know it and those who do hide it in a tomb-like silence, except the brazen, the headlongly honest, and the artlessly frank. I come under none of those heads. I am myself. I live and ponder alone.

And my Body feels consciously aloof and as a someway separate individual: with inner organs as eternal hopes, smooth skin as emotion, and drops of blood as thoughts - little drops of sparkling red virile sweet blood for its thoughts.

I so *love* my Body as it lives and breathes and moves about, with me and close to me. It is my so constant companion. It is an attractive girl, a human being of some charm. I love it for the priceless air it breathes and the long jewel-days of sunshine it has known: for the tiny wears and tears of its daily life - the rending of its magic tissues with each going-up-or-down-stairs, each crossing of a door-sill.

I love it for that it must lie at last pale, pale and still - still - still - in its grave.

I love my Body for its woman-complexities of sex.

I love it for the lonely lyric poetry of its cell-adventures.

I love my Body for this long journey of woe and loveliness which it goes, from Birthday to Deathday, in wilding passions of subtle nervousness: each day a day of bodily beauty and intolerableness and fear and utter mystery: because life *is*, and because I own a white smooth-skinned Body, and because the strange, strange Air of Everyday breathes on it - touches it - always!

*

Sincerity and Despair

To-morrow

I am a true Artist, not as a writer but as a writing-person. I try to feel myself literarily a poet - finer-made than a god. But I fail as a poet-*litterateur* as I fail as a poet-person. A poet flies always on wings of fiery gold though it might be waywardly. But often I walk with my feet in odd gutters, and have some plaisance in them, and analyze their gutteriness absorbedly and own them as part of my portion.

- poet or no poet, it is best to be myself. In heights and murks and widths and trivial horrors, myself -

But as an Artist I am in the true. As a painter of words and maker of paragraphs which picture my phases and emotions, and in my conscious feeling anent it, I realize the artist *flair*, the artist temper.

It is not a literary but a personal art.

I have what goes with all artist-matter - long periods of dry-rot when having nothing ripe to write I write nothing. My Artist-spirit proves itself, justifies itself in my times of stagnation and reaction. Out of it something human and sad and lustrous grows in me, something which is half worldly but awaits its ripe time of expression with someway-divine scorn.

I once thought me destined to be a "writer" in the ordinary sense. And many good people visioned a writing career for me. It has a vapid taste, just to recall it. My flawed life has that to felicitate upon - that I have not spent it in fat lumps of writing, magazine tales and sex-novels. In the days, and later, when my *demi-vierge* book made its success I was besought by publishers to write others - to go on, to reap and garner. I pushed all that away with a preoccupied hand, not as part and parcel of my wastrel living but in my assured Artist-temper.

I should feel more true-to-form to earn my living by making linen roses in a shop, along with rows of pale women, than by my writing.

My writing to me is a precious thing - and a rare bird - and a Babylonish jade. It demands gold in exchange for itself. But though it is my talent it is not my living. It is too myself, like my earlobes and my throat, to commercialize by the day.

But I can not think of me as an Artist without thinking of me as a Liar. The two are someway related. I am an appalling, an encompassing Liar. I am a Liar by the clock. My life ticks out silent lies as my little clock ticks out seconds. It is a phase hard to put my finger on. I feel it on me the way I feel a headache. I write this book with seriousness and earnestness. It is all a mood of sincerity and despair. But except I give it some backgrounding of lies, though each thing in it is fair fact, I fail as an Artist.

It is strange about lies - any lies, all lies. They are muscularly stronger than truths. They come more readily to human tongues. They fit more easily into the games of this life. And in me they seem needful to my Artist mind.

I mean not the lies I may tell but the lies I think.

I mean not my falseness. That is a different thing, one I feel someway responsible for. But the thinking lies feel to be a heritage from ancient evil selves.

I lie to myself, to the air around me - I blow lies into space from my quiet lips. And one half of me knows them for lies and the other half of me *believes* them.

Those half-known lies, the *need* of the lies half-believed, are the realization of an essential Artist-spirit.

The oblique belief in them and the recognition of them as lies proclaim me to myself, as a writing-person: Liar and Artist.

*

It's Not Death

To-morrow

It's not Death I fear, nor Life.

I horridly fear something this side of Death but out-pacing Life a little: a nervousness in my Stomach - a very Muddy Street - a Lonely Hotel Room.

*

A Human Prerogative

To-morrow

It is a quiet deep of night. A bell has just tolled two.

I am clothed in cool bedroom negligeés and a softening sweetness of cold cream, from head to foot.

I am tranquil for to-day I had a walk that made me feel Sincere and Safe.

It is a comforting feeling: it is like a beef-sandwich.

It was a long walk south-east of Butte along an outskirting road where I used often to walk when I was sixteen - a broad gray desert. It was the same sand and barrenness. It was bare and withered as if a giant coyote had picked its rocky ribs.

The day was windy and dusty. The sunshine was thick and sweet and heavy like floating honey. The dust that blew against the white of my neck was like ground glass.

My feet ached as I walked.

My shoes were Cuban-heeled thick-soled pumps of corded silk, a kind easy to walk in. But the same feet which once readily bore me seven miles along that road ache now at three. All of me ached as I walked along. I cursed desultorily with a smooth whispered flow of curses, because the circumstances seemed to demand it. But I loved the walk - even the more for my tired feet and my aching knees and my irking drooping shoulders and the hot glazed sand against my throat.

My Soul tasted realness in it.

Quite close to me, in immense sad beauty, were the deep high heavy silent somber hills of Montana. To-day the nearer ones were a stately enchanted Blue: a Blue of all ages: a Blue of infinitude: a Blue with a feel of life and death in its Blueness. Above it the sky was not blue but a pale glimmering shimmering silver hung across with gray silk clouds soft as doves' plumage.

I sat on a flat rock and looked at all of it and at the desert around, and at my dusty shoes.

All of it felt overwhelmingly sincere: at one with the wide worn used earth.

My dusty shoes looked to be at one with it and could interpret it.

I felt my shoes could claim their human prerogative of getting dusty in any of this world's roads.

It gave me a feeling of human Sincerity: good-and-evil Safeness.

It is on me now, along with cold cream and strong memory of Desert and Sun and Blue.

It is as good as a beef-sandwich.

Better: I don't like beef-sandwich.

*

The Merciless Beauty

To-morrow

Sometimes the dusk is full of fire.

Some dusks I sit by my window looking out and hotly and coldly want a Lover: hotly with my Body and coldly with my Mind.

A dusk has just gone. I sat looking out at it.

A mist of dark cream tinged with heated violet came from nowhere and hung above the ground.

Suddenly came on me a sense of bewildering mysterious beauty.

In it was a feel of rippling warmth that crept into my bone-and-flesh from forehead to heel, from temples to soles, from crown to toe-tips.

It crept slow and suffocating like magic chloroform.

I leaned elbows on window-sill and chin on palms and sunk my gaze in the violet shades outside and straightway knew I wanted a Lover: not in delicate moonlit culmination like Juliet in her balcony: not denyingly like the timid young nun in her cloister assailed unaware by faint forbidden emotions.

I wanted a Lover like the jungle leopard leaping through the Springtime covert at nightfall to find her mate.

It is a subtle and an obvious feeling, made of a merciless beauty.

It is the tired urge of sex-tissues and nerve-cells: positive, furious, fiery as the bloodiest sun. It is the same which the heated leopard feels in her sharp immaculate lust. It is quite the same - but it could not move me as I sat alone loverless to the knitting of an eyebrow, to a change of posture, a movement of elbows on the window-sill or of palms beneath my chin. Nor could it, though the potential Lover had stood outside my window.

For any woman of any charm the world is full of Lovers: each and all to be had by the flutter of her finger, the droop of her white eyelids, the trembling of her pink-bowed lips. The world is full of them - facile Lovers, craven, potent, and pinchbeck. And it's that kind I want hotly with my Body, coldly with my Mind in dusks of rippling warmth - rippling, rippling warmth -

I want the Lover as the leopard wants hers. But I'm not a leopard: instead, a woman-person of keen sentientness and wild wistful imagination. So I wouldn't so much as crook a finger to call a Lover to me: a curious nervous inertia.

It's only I *want* the Lover with frantic blind cosmic ardors inside me.

I analyze it in my magic Mind and find I would call no Lover. I analyze farther and find I'd reject all but an impossible one-in-ten-thousand. But remains the desire, hot as live embers, cold as hail.

Sex is an odd attribute. It has been to me like a blest impediment and a celestial incumbrance and a radiant curse. -

When I was seventeen I stood on a threshold and peered curiously into a dim-lit strange-scented Room.

It was unknown to me then. My mind alone bespoke it. As I stood at its doorway the air it wafted out touched my sense with only the lightest frayed-cobweb contact, unintelligible and unenlightening. I had lived an emptily alone girlhood. I was icily virginal.

At five-and-twenty I crossed the Room's threshold. I breathed lightly the odd fragrance. I looked curiously around. I touched some amorous-looking grapes and some love-promising apples that lay about: I bit into one and burst a grape with my finger and thumb. I gathered a weak-petaled flower or two. I gauged the Room and its furnishments and was unthrilled by anything in it. Even bodily it left me unthrilled.

Those two memory-mists do not keep me in the now-dusk and in the strength and terror and fire of top-most youth from wanting a sudden Lover with all that's in my Body.

Love has naught to do with it. Love is a flame-winged Bird. I know it. I know the values of my life and of me. I do not mistake tapers for torches, ducats for louis d'ors, vicarious nepenthe for dreamless death.

In dusk-moments my bone-and-flesh is all of me I'm sure of. It begins and ends in this earth. It answers the violent summonses of this earth and its dusks.

In the just-gone dusk I felt the prickling blood flow to my finger-ends. A flood-tide, blinding red, surged and seethed and bubbled and pounded at my heart.

"I want a Lover - some Lover" - I murmured to the shadows beyond my window.

I grew breathless.

The spirit of my flesh rose like a wind-blown flame.

A loud cry rang in my nerve-wilderness.

That moment the variant analysis which always rides with me stopped dead.

There came instead sheer feeling - the merciless beauty.

- a man-person, maybe - the man of happy unanalytic brutality - to be suddenly there with me: to flash into my shadowy solitude like a lightning bolt and burst and break me

- a quarter-hour of exquisite wildness - restlessness, made of Star-flame and Lily-petal and Cloud-burst on Mountain-summits and Sea-waves purple in a Stormy Dawn - an intolerable hunger and ecstasy -

But just gone and I sit writing it in the pale cast of thought.
But breathlessly I recall the breathlessness of it.

*

My Shoes

To-morrow

I love my Shoes.

I love them because they so guard my feet.

I walk many a mile along the stone pavements and into distant odd streets and on open roads at the outskirts of this Butte.

And while I walk I think.

I think things of a great many kinds - potent and magic and mad. The act of walking starts an engine in my sparkling infernal mind. And the weight and the sting and the hurt and the fascination of my walking thoughts bear down on my slim feet as they carry me along. And the hard-beaten world beneath them feels resentful and uncomplaisant to my soles.

And then I look down at my Shoes with their trim tailored vamps and their walk-worthy soles and instantly my feet feel secure against evil, smartly protected from my thoughts and from the world's surface: my thoughts which shoot down on them out of my devilish brain and the world-hardness beneath them.

To-day I was walking along the road that leads up the ever-wonderful Anaconda Hill - a place of stones and sand-wastes and hoists and scaffoldings and mines with ten thousand digging men thousands of feet down in their metallic bowels. Close by were melancholy mulberry-toned mountains at the north-east. They were tragic, triumphant, grief-stricken, terrifyingly beautiful. Purple clouds hung around them like mourning veils. I can't look enough at those - it is as if there weren't enough looking-power in my human gray eyes.

Presently I came to a small open space as I walked, a toy desert. A toy desert is more like a desert than is a real one. The sand in it is grayer sand. The stones are abrupter. The sun is flatter-looking. The air is less willing to furnish breath to a human being. The best that could be said of this one is that it was intolerably desolate. I looked about and about it. And suddenly I was afraid. Afraid of many things: afraid of grief-stricken mountains: afraid of my life and of Me.

I leaned against a yellow ledge of rock with a subtle sickening faintish feeling. "I am afraid," I said inside me, "of this world and this life, and of all things little and large - nerves and Christmas days and poetry: toy deserts and all. How can I cope with it - I alone?"

Then I looked down at my Shoes of black soft dull leather and cloth, buttoned snugly around my ankles and with tough supple soles fit to take me to Jericho and back. Thus neatly armored I felt suddenly my blue-veined feet need fear nothing from sand and stone and hardness of ground. And if my feet are not afraid - my feet which bear weights of all-of-me - why should afraidness touch my spirit which is proud?

There will be always Shoes in the world: stout stylish serviceable boots, and pale delicate rat-skin pumps, and satin mule-slippers.

And always I shall have Shoes: in toy deserts I shall have black strong snug-buttoned ones.

I looked at them in this toy-desert and straightway I wasn't afraid.

It has been often like that.

So I love my Shoes.

An Eerie Quality

To-morrow

When I was Ten years old I played marbles "for keeps," smoked little pieces of rattan buggy-whip in the hay-scented barn and slid "belly-buster" down long winter hills on my sled. And I hammered and sawed ruinously with grownup tools, whistling happily. And I played with dolls absorbedly for hours on end.

I was not boyish and not girlish.

I was not childish except for an oddly hungry child-heart.

I was myself.

So long ago and longer I consciously owned an eerie quality which toppled over the edge of my humanness.

And still own it.

*

A Helliad

To-morrow

This noonday as I sat on the veranda two young lads stopped by the stone coping which borders this front yard, and conversed. One was eager-looking and about eleven years old. The other was perhaps thirteen and morose and he had a small rifle which he polished with a bit of waste, not lifting his gaze as they talked.

Said the younger boy: "Say-Frank, I could'a had that old shot-gun off my dad if I'd'a went after it to Rocker that time."

"Like hell you could," said Frank.

"Say-Frank, you know that Winchester o' Billy O'Rourke's? - he made six bull's-eyes and one inside ring with it day 'fore yesterday."

"Like hell he did," said Frank.

"Say-Frank, Mexicans and Indians can get a guy ev'ry time with a long-distance rifle without taking aim through the sight."

"Like hell they can," said Frank.

"Say-Frank, there's a kid down on South Arizona that's got a Colt automatic that'll hit without him aiming at all."

"Like hell there is," said Frank.

"Say-Frank, you know them little brass machine-guns the militia's got? - the bores o' them things're rifled just like this."

"Like hell they are," said Frank.

"Say-Frank, my grandfather in Illinois's got a bullet in him he got at the battle o' Fredricksburg in the Civil War."

"Like hell he has," said Frank.

"Say-Frank, it costs a hundred thousand dollars to make a Krupp gun and eighty dollars ev'ry time you fire it."

"Like hell it does," said Frank.

"Say-Frank, it ain't a felony to croak a burglar with a gun even if he's only breakin' into somebody else's house."

"Like hell it ain't," said Frank.

"Say-Frank, my mother goes huntin', too - she can shoot rabbits and ducks on the wing and once she got a deer with that big old .44 o' my Uncle Walt's."

"Like hell she did," said Frank.

"Say-Frank - listen, will you gimme your gun for my bicycle, both my catcher's gloves, and four dollars when I get paid?"

"Like hell I will," said Frank.

"Say-Frank - listen, will you gimme it for my bicycle, my two catcher's gloves, four dollars when I get paid, and my shepherd pup?"

"Like hell I will," said Frank.

"Say-Frank - listen, - and my artificial snake?"

"Like hell," said Frank.

"Say-Frank - listen, - and my half o' Ernest's camera?"

"Like hell," said Frank.

"Say-Frank - listen, - and my last year's shin-guards?"

"Like hell," said Frank.

"Say-Frank - *listen*, - and my *this* year's shin-guards?"

"Like *hell*," said Frank.

"Say-Frank, come right down to it I don't want a .22. If I get a gun this year it'll be a .32."

"Like he -" -

Which point I felt to be the top-note of the helliad, so I rose and came into the house.

I felt replete with rhythm and with a sense of surprising human attitudes remote from my own.

*

Swift Go My Days

To-morrow

Swift, Swift go my days.

By rights I think time should drag with me, for I am wasting my portion of life as I live it.

But my days pass Swift - Swift, Swift.

They come, they fly away - before I know.

I'm thinking it is Tuesday: but while I'm thinking - Wednesday has come: and gone: and Thursday is rushing in. Tuesday, blue-and-gold or gray-and-silver, with its mornings and nights and bits of food and openings of doors and thinkings: Wednesday with the same equipment: Thursday the same.

Each day comes and goes like a flash of filmed silvered garbled light.

But there is time in each for me to touch the enchanted Everydayness: time for the turbulent sly delight of tasting, smelling, feeling the eternal humors and romances in each small thing near me - my Clock, my Window, my Jar of Cold Cream, my Two Thumbs. There is time in each day for it to make me pay a wearing glimmering feverish homage to the mystic daily godhead.

My life exacts terrific homages from me.

I am wearing out - frailly, tiredly, from a desolate uneasy love of living.

It is why my days go Swift when by rights time should drag leadenly in punishment for barbarous futileness.

There is not time-space enough in any of the days sufficient to love the virile green and the murderous red and the sweet pale surprising purple in the sunset above the west desert: nor space to love the smell of a sudden August rain: nor the flaming delicate Idea of the poet John Keats.

While I'm starting to love each of those to its height of love-worthiness - the to-day is gone: and the to-morrow, which must see a new love-game started for each Thing, is come.

But while I say "is come": it's gone.

So Swift go my days - oh Swift, Swift!

*

By the Blood of Dead Americans

To-morrow

Since I wrote the beginning of this there has come the war in Europe: a war full of suffering brave women and dead children: full of German greed and cruelty and stupidity and of French gameness and cheerfulness, French splendor of valor.

It has an effect of some kind on each person who reads so much as its "headlines."

It has the effect on me of making me a jealously patriotic American.

It makes me think of Lexington and Gettysburg with an odd furious personal shame.

We are Americans not by accident but by the blood of dead Americans. But we assume it is by accident.

We lie down like a nation of bastards to let the pig-hearted Hun trample by proxy on our neck.

It was for America to declare war in the same hour the *Lusitania* passengers met murder. We were not "too proud" but afraid. Afraid and not ready.

Not ready has no right thing to do with it.

They were not ready at Lexington.

I long with some passion to exchange my two black dresses for two white ones with red crosses on the sleeves: to serve my country in a day of death and honor.

It too is all the time under my skin though I write along but in this flawed song of myself.

*

To Express Me

To-morrow

I suppose I'm very lonely.

It is luck - luck from the stars - not to be beset by clusters of people, people who do their thinking outside their heads, "cheerful" people, people who say "pardon me": all the damning sorts scattered about obstructing one's view of the horizons.

But for want of - other, *other* people - I am intensely lonely.

When I was eighteen I thought I must be the most lonely creature in this world. I analyzed my life then as now and it by itself had set me apart. But I stood then as it's given Youth to stand - on High Ground. I was strong to endure loneliness while viciously hating it.

There was unaware a hope-colored bliss in my inexperience which companioned me. I felt it then without knowing I felt it. I can see that plainly now.

Now also I see plainly and feel plainly that I stand on lower ground, at poorer vantage. As my bodily strength which was then robust is now slight. The metaphysic life-shadows reach me more easily. They have a feel of fatally shutting down, fatefully closing in. They are the mirages on the dun-colored worldly air near me of my own useless untoward selves. There is no more the hope-colored bliss.

At eighteen I said to me: "I'm lonely but some day I may be happily friendshiped and apprehended and it will be like paradise."

Now I say to me: "I'm lonely by fate and by nature and temperament. I've known some friendships of vivid alluringness and informingness - they await me now in the offing. And others. There *is* paradise in it - an odd sweet dubious paradise. But what's the use - ?"

It's that what's-the-use, born of the lower vantage-ground and the closing-in shadows, that chiefly makes me lonely - lonely to a desperateness and on through to a ruinous calm.

It is this metaphysic loneliness which breeds in me one constant reason-less restless urgent motif: to Express me: not of-the-past except desultorily, not of-the-future save indifferently: but of my low-toned, low-echoing now. Until I've Expressed me there's no setting open the gates of my spirit to a passer-by, though the passer-by should be a poet-in-the-flesh, a god, an angel with a torch.

Four-and-twenty turbulent moods may break over me in a day, or four-and-twenty passive ones, or four-and-twenty someway joyous ones. But like the theme in a fugue this loud tranquil recurrent need to Express me transcends them all.

It is a big voracious part-human bird of prey. Of it too I say what's-the-use. But it is a need without a use, a need scornful of use. It springs unconceived, unsourced from inside me. It rises from the ashes of blightingest moods and beats its bruising strong wings against my face.

It says: "Know me, defer to me, Slim-woman. Serve me, follow me, gather-in all your answers for me. Do this though I undo you, though I rend you, tear you with my sharp teeth so like a wolf's. When you've answered me I may let you go. Until then, turn to me. Tell me: tell me again and again. Utter yourself. Interpret. Unfold."

It makes my life-space someway sweet, someway heartbreaking, someway frightful - strewn with dust of broken stars.

I live long hours of nervous profound passionate self-communion. I discover strange lovely age-worn facets of my Soul. I discover the subtle panting Ego - the wonderful thing that lives and waits in its garbled radi-ance just beneath my skin.

To ask oneself and make answer out of oneself is the most delicious of this life's mental delectations. I might have missed it but for those beating bruising wings against my face, now and years ago: for expressing breeds the last Expressions.

I might have gone on through years and decades and lumps of months knowing at best a little of some rare person, a little less or more of another rare person, a little of a musician's soul in a nocturne, a little of a dead poet's splendors. But to Me and my own fine spirit-relationships to those things I could remain, but for my radiant flawed egotistic interpreting, eternally strange.

But for it I'd not have the wit to perceive the one human being in the world I may know with vitalness: my own Self. I should drop into my grave at last without a good-by to the glowing one who was locked just inside, whose hand I'd never clasped, whose sad prescient eyes I'd never looked in, who was then flitting out and on and away.

It is a being cruel and transfiguring and terrifying: terribly worth clasping close and breathing with.

And some days it sleeps, sleeps like the dead: it is delicater than rose-vapors before the dawn: a sun-blown faëry thing.

When it sleeps I'm left alone. Then comes a doubtful dreadful quiet, a hell of dumbness that only God could reach.

It is as if neither God nor I attempts to cope with it.

*

Bastard Lacy Valentines

To-morrow

The thing I admire most is strength. The thing I most hate is Weakness, of each and every kind.

All the reassuring things in the world are in and of the strong deeds done in it. All the mischief and despair come from human Weakness.

I would better strongly murder my foe than forgive him Weakly for my seeming advantage. I would be happier in my mind as a careful charwoman than as a loose-jointed poet. I would rather have a farthing's value as a faithful concubine than no value as a slattern housewife.

Strength repays itself with strength - and with magnificence.

Truth is strength nearly always: and *not* always. To cheat strongly in the life-game gets me more than does Weak easy honesty. By being a strong man Napoleon brought home the bacon. Being an honest one would have got him not one rasher of the bacon of *his* desire. The race is too ridden with "temperament" to let truth be its prevailing force. But strength plows its scornful way through temperament like a steam-shovel. The bacon Napoleon brought home he took from other people, causing them misery. They were Weak and let him take it, or they were strong and got killed trying to keep it. To get killed trying to keep your bacon is to be even stronger than the Napoleon who lives and takes it from you. Those who sit still and *let* Napoleon get their bacon are fit only to be themselves made into bacon.

Truth belongs with love, with friendship, with charity, with psychic lovingkindness: with all the altruistic graces and tendernesses.

But in the mere grinding livingness of things it is to be strong. I say to Me, "Mary MacLane, be strong: whether you're living joyous on a hill or mournful in a valley, make shift to be strong."

In which paragraphs I make an apologetic preamble to Me when about to dwell on my odd ironic element of Weakness. My Weakness is not an art nor a science nor a gift nor a trait but is a sort of ruinous trade touched with all of those, a trade at which I work and lose heavily from a viewpoint of personal economy.

In Atlanta-Georgia lives a man with whom I exchange semi-occasional letters. He is thirty-nine and clever and what is called a business man. He is a business man not only by circumstance but by nature. At a glance one would picture him in the setting of an office in a steel-and-brick building with a roll-top desk, a swivel chair, a cabinet full of files, a stenographer with an unregenerate vocabulary, and stationery neatly engraved with his name, his business, his cable address, and his telephone number. The look of the neat letterhead and the fibrous feel of the bond paper give one the idea that whoever went into a business venture with him would come out of it disadvantageously.

After another glance at himself one would infer that his leisure hours might be fancifully spent. In hours of ease some business men follow baseball, others golf, "tired" ones musical comedy. Others take up curio collecting or some personal phantasm. In the latter category is my acquaintance of Atlanta. He affects Mary MacLane and musings of her in his leisure hours. But what I am to him does not concern nor much interest me. What he is to me concerns me, for he - his letters - are a present source of my elaborated Weakness.

I feel a wave of conscious Weakness washing over me as I write about it. His letters make a soft buffer, a foolish pretty window, a tinted veil between me and my too-harsh actualities.

I met him when I lived in New York. He had read the book I wrote in the early nineteen-hundreds and at meeting me he conceived a thinly insistent admiration which someway went to his head. He has at intervals since then written me letters full of charmed and salubrious flattery and of appreciation and praise for traits and gifts and qualities which I do not possess. They appeal and cater remarkably to my vanity - and are pleasant and unreal and vain and fatuous and fond and piquant.

He is a clever man and does not make love to me. A butcher's-boy may write love-letters - and I'd prefer those of a butcher's-boy to those of a business man: they would be more sincere and less hopelessly discreet. But this business man is discerning and intuitive and writes me no love. His wife - a business man always has a wife - could not rationally object to what is in the letters, though she would irrationally and naturally object to the letters themselves. She is unloving and unloved - they always are - but whatever may be her caste (I know only that she is tall and blonde and named Bertha) she doubtless would find something superfluous in the idea of her husband's letters to me.

A letter comes from him in Georgia after I have written him a brief disquieting one with a latent human appeal in it to make him think the chief thing I need in life is his appreciation, his attitude toward me, to brace my spirit. Then his comes, written in his small slanting commercial hand. It is arresting from any angle and well thought, well couched.

In it he tells me that my brain, scintillantly brilliant though it is, needs the dim twilights of other brains such as his to catch the sparks it throws off.

Which is a lie. My brain is not scintillantly brilliant and it "needs" nothing. But the lie is agreeable to read. There is a gentle caressingness in its untruth which feels someway soothinger than any flattering fact.

And he tells me my chief attraction as an individual is my ability accurately to gauge another individual and to breathe myself graciously out to it and upon it while pretending to be immersed in my own ego.

Which is another lie. Immersed in my own ego is never a pretense with me, and I have not gauged - in the sense of weighing and measuring - another individuality except to hate it. But it is piquantly restful to hear that I am thus benign.

And he tells me that though several years have passed since he and I took leave of one another he has never forgotten that last parting because it was like the passing of a little weir-woman who brushed him lightly with her garments as she went.

Which is another lie. My association with him was in brief meetings at hectic studio tea-fights and two noisy dinners at Churchill's, at all of which I frowned impatiently at his tiresome conversation. And his leave-taking with me consisted in his sharpening a lead-pencil - beautifully he sharpened it - for me to write a telegram with. It was not until this correspondence that we established an unreliable intimacy. But to be told I seemed a weir-woman to a hard-headed business man who could doubtless cheat a client out of four thousand dollars easily in a half-day's maneuvering is oddly inspiriting.

And he tells me he is highly privileged to be permitted to gaze in at the mezzo-tinted windows of my soul, which are surely curtained against the passing proletariat.

Which is another lie. He has never remotely glimpsed my tired Soul in the firmly false little letters I've written him. As to its being a privilege if he had: it is the proletariat, it so happens, who have first chance at those windows, which are not mezzo-tinted but made of the plainest of plain glass. But the conceit tastes mellow and naif and bromidic and appetizing to me, like cream and raspberries in July.

And he tells me the most delightful thing in the world would be to live near me and have a season of daily meetings - meetings of astral selves upon a "higher plane" whereon we should exchange those flowers and fruits of the spirit which grow not from the soils but from the esoteric essences of life: - that sort of thing.

Which is another lie. No possible man (except a Poet whom I loved - or perhaps a scientist -) could find me delightful for more than two consecutive meetings - I develop something like temper - and I care for no higher planes except in airships. As for esoterics, I would fainer exchange musings anent over-shoes than over-souls. And my spirit bears in fertile earthy soil chiefly thistles from which men gather no figs. But it gives me a warmish feeling, similar to a hot-water bottle between my shoulders on a winter night, to read that picturesque palaver written to me in my slim scorn by him in his springy swivel chair.

Thus it goes. His letters are made all of softest quaintest lies which I know to be lies the moment my gray gaze falls on them. All his premises in regard to me and his deductions from them are roundly lightly mistaken. But I like that fluent flattery the more because it is so false. I am too vain a creature to want to cope often with truths even though they might be uplifting self-lauding truths. My vain peculiar Weakness demands as well semi-occasional collations of creamed lies upon which it feeds like a sleek cat on creamed fish. My humor enters into it, in no obvious way but eerily like a gay ghost. My humor is a strong influence in me. It is stronger than my pride and anger and fear and caution and reverence and self-love - stronger than most things I own.

And it's for reasons of pastime and vanity and oblique humor I let letters from the business man come, though not often, into my solitudes. And I spend hours of inert time-waste conning his fanciful ideas. And the letters I write him in reply, though brief and impersonal and done in my best false manner, consume a surprising lot of time and mental and physical force to write. It is the Weakness in it which is so devouring: it eats me hungrily and lingers about like a buzzard, picking my bones.

A spinelessly Weak game. I hate its Weakness more than I like its pleasant futility. I hate it and myself in it all the time I'm dwelling on it. I hate it as I'd hate a little drug habit fastened on my nerves.

Its influence is the same but more insidious than a drug would be, more demoralizing. As feeling fear makes one afraid, feeling more fear makes one more afraid.

Still once in a month, once in a two-month, I feel the hankering itch to be applauded for second-rate qualities I do not own, and I give way to it: in a particularly Weak way, after my sanest self has reduced it analytically to shreds, and after saying bosh! with all my selves.

After telling Me too that it is a common-tasting game. Life is a strange music-clangor of gold bells, some silent, some far-echoing. And the common-tasting thing cracks a bell-edge.

Then briskly I answer the last letter from Atlanta-Georgia and soon there comes a fresh sheaf of smooth velvetish lies to pad my way.

There may come no more if this I write now should find its way to Atlanta-Georgia. Or if fate or Bertha should intervene.

But always I know Weakness of me will find ways to work at its losing trade.

It is of the dubious inevitable side of human nature - like gold teeth and tinned salmon and bastard lacy valentines.

*

Sweet Fine Sweatings of Blood

To-morrow

Merely from the view-point of outward intellect this book of myself is oddly difficult to write.

My most-loved thing to do and my hardest thing to do is to write.

It is hard to catch and hold with mental fingers one's own emotions and then doubly hard to write them.

A feeling is something without the words and without even the thought. To put it into the thought and then into the words is a minuter task than would be the translating of a Francois-Villon poem into Choctaw.

It's a knowing person who realizes her own emotions and a knowinger who recognizes what is what, who is who, which is which among them. I look inward at Me and I see an emotion of World-Weariness and want to write it. I write it as nearly as I can. But when I have done - it's not World-Weariness that I wrote but its twin sister, Boredom-of-the-Moment, which happened to be next the other when I looked.

I am glad to have transcribed Boredom-of-the-Moment. It is the finer and thinner and more elusive of the two. But how and why did I fail of World-Weariness?

But sometime when I aim at Fear or Resentment or Surprise it may be World-Weariness I'll bring down unexpectedly with a clean wing-shot.

When I set out to write the Look-in-my-Eyes it may be the Feel-of-my-Fingers that comes out in my round writing. Another time I think I'm writing my Bad-Tooth: until I get it written when it turns out to be my little Eye-Wrinkles.

Having failed of the thought often I fail of the words.

When I have a particularly M.-Mac-Lane thought to express I review the top tier of my vocabulary of words to find proper ones for it. They are all very nice words in that top-tier - neatly washed and dressed and hair-brushed and tidied-up, like the children in a small private school: words like Necessary and Irresolute and Crockery and Inconvenience and Broth and Apprise: good words and useful if one's thought is radical or risky and wants conserving. I call some of them to me and question them and consider them and ponder a bit, and decide they will none of them suit. Then I go to the bottom tier, the unkemptest of words in the untidiest attire: words like Traipse and Nab and Glim and Hennery and Chape and Plash. And I at once reject those as too carelessly bred for my terse thoughts to associate with. (But for my uncombed ungroomed grimy-faced thoughts I turn to them.) Then I glance over a tier of mysterious words, spruce but with inde-finable vagabond faces: such as Whelk and Mauger and Frush and Gnurl and Yare and Hyaline. They are expressive but of a kind it's well to use with caution, the kind that may trip up thoughts that would make them their medium and lead to slips 'twixt cups and lips. So I dismiss them with a mental reservation of one or two to use if I fail to find right ones among the less mysterious. Then I turn to a tier that represents the virile middle-class in words, the lower-case words, the mob and riot words, the words for poets and anarchists and prophets: such as Adroit and Nightingale and Gallows and Gutter and Woman and Madrigal and Death. And I say, "Without doubt here are my words." But I use discretion. I know that tier of words to be of the nature of bombs, of strychnine, of a dynamic force resistible against all human and worldly substance. They also must be used cautiously and with a sparing hand. With caution one can handle a bomb, and sparingly one can eat strychnine, and one can control any dynamic force by studying its tendencies and keeping out of its direct road. It behooves one to heed those conditions in broaching the counter-mining counter-irritant words if one would avoid blowing oneself analytically broadcast.

So I may have found the right sort of words and measured their pos-sibilities and pitfalls. But again: it's a nerve-racking task to choose out one word from seven, one from five, one from two. I see two words which may be the only proper ones out of ten thousand to bear my thought. The two may be Echo and After-glow, each an unacknowledged half-sister to the other: meaning respectively something living and growing and vibrant in my spirit-ears and fading and dying and radiant before my spirit-eyes. But because my spirit-ears may glow bright and hot from what they heard, or my spirit-eyes may seem to themselves to gaze a moment at a soundless sound - an Unheard Melody of Keats, - I miss the raylike distinction and I write After-glow when my true word was Echo.

But another time I write Echo perfectly and masterfully to my own delight: having meant After-glow.

So it is. There's no plain sailing on this analytic sea. And if there were it would be not worth while. I want nothing, nothing, nothing that comes easily. What comes easily I distrust, be it love or language. It afterward proves dead-sea fruit. What I suffer to get I know to be life-food even if it drugs or pains or poisons me. It is one lesson I have learned.

Without doubt it is so with everybody, all around. One sees only surfaces, husks. Anyone looking casually at this Me sitting writing might say, - "How easily and smoothly and well she writes. How kind of God to give her so light a task in life. How complacently go her working hours." And I looking casually at, oh, Miss Lily Walker singing and swaying and glancing sideways in a gorgeous Broadway chorus - I might say, "How easy a task in life has *that* brainless gazelle. To work with her body, and not even with the sweats and sinews of it like a scrub-woman, and not with the facile shames of it like a lorette, but with the grace and suppleness and beauty and suggestions of it, aided by a soprano throat and a soprano face - with only the effort it wants to fling it all over footlights. And that pastime gets her her livelihood."

But whoever marks me writing as one doing an easy task because I write along rapidly enough considers nothing of my mental travail for the thought, my blind grope for the language, my little nervous anguish of choice among the double-edged and triple-pronged words: and the neat concise failure of the result.

And no, I do not thus comment on Miss Lily Walker. I have an appreciative pleasure in her charm and suppleness and bird-and-butterfly prettiness. But after a bit of contemplation and analysis of her surface I deduce the unconscious struggle it may be for Miss Lily Walker to be supple on nights when she does not feel supple, the thin agony of being sweet when she does not feel sweet, the neurotic torture of being seductive *regularly* - by the night: the more that perchance the struggle always *is* unconscious. Her brain being required in her body it's to be assumed there's none in her head. But I can deduce a nervous red heart beating illogically somewhere in her being protesting dumbly sometimes against one irking item, sometimes against another, sometimes against all the items in Miss Lily Walker's scheme of life, but beating and beating on, like a little automatic drum wound up tight and tossed into a maelstrom to beat itself out.

I'd like - like with breathless eagerness - to read the analyzed being just beneath Miss Lily Walker's skin.

Everybody - every human being - is wildly *Real*: radiant and desolate. -

With no amount of temperamental struggling could Miss Lily Walker analyze a psychic emotion of her own and then find the right word-combination to write it in.

With no conceivable effort of mine could I manage to be supple when I do not feel supple.

So Miss Lily Walker and I are quits at this game.

It totals up evenly, all ways around.

Nobody gets through one Real day - though it be a dayful of Real lies - without a demoniacal struggle of soul or a heavy blow on the personal solar plexus.

And I make not even the intellect side of this book, which is a Realness to me, without sweet fine sweatings of blood.

*

Instinct - A "First Law"

To-morrow

I long to do a Murder.

Despite my futile way-of-life and my rotting destroying half-acquiescence in it I have a furious positive Murder in me.

One near me in my daily life injures me and goes on injuring me in a way which is scourging and malicious and intensely petty. There is in it helpless humiliation for me - me self-loving, proud, and determinedly unsuppliant - and it makes maddening Murder rise in me.

I don't know why I do not do the Murder. I have nothing to lose by paying the law-penalty: nothing but my life, and my life is stripped bare - and was always barren by God's decree - of all that makes a life sacred or lovely or precious. For long years and years, since child-days, I have been lost.

I don't know why I do not do the Murder: except that I think of it and brood over it and turn it round and round smoulderingly in my Mind. From no choice. I have tried to push the feeling away as a common thing beneath me. It is beneath me, for I am not little but someway big. But my

Mind will take its toll of all that confronts me.

The humiliation and the helplessness to combat being humiliated in me who keep a casual proudness toward people is like a secret hot sword thrust, and kept freshly thrust, in my flesh. It makes me wild to do the Murder. But it makes me brood over it till the red act is lost in red brooding.

There come also thinkings.

Murder, any Murder, is in its essence cowardly, a slinking meanness. And I am not cowardly and I am not mean. I am above malice and retaliation - all such impoverished impoverishing emotions. A shrug of my shoulders and they are satisfied. The impulse to hit back after a bitter wound is not of vengeance. It is instinct - a "first law." But Murder is self-accusingly cowardly and sneakingly human. I can't get away from that. To take away a person's life is like setting fire to his house - an officiously stooping act. It's for me to live my life in aloof self-sufficience. No human malice should reach me in it. Then it's not for me to reach out of it and stain my good fingers with unpleasant sticky blood. I am always in a prison of radiance and gloom.

But the mere habit of being a human being is breakingly insistent - no matter how many or how few frocks one owns. Neither of my two dresses is a protection against humiliation. A thin black serge dress gives me to myself a melancholy cold inert air: but beneath the smooth-fitting breast of it comes too often a throbbing frightful to feel, frightful to know, made of fierce petty anger and abasing hurt. I hide it and me in my room and twist my hands together and walk my floor, and a hurricane of helpless bitter trifling woe shakes and wrenches me. Then Murder enters me.

What humiliates me is an obvious common thing that to any human one would mean hurt and more hurt. Though I am determinedly brave I am sensitive.

I do not write itself because this is the book of me and not of people.

It is a slight, a poor and vivid cruelness. There is the tie of blood in it which in all ways - from a deep heritage - I respect: and it rubs an added stinging poison in the wound.

It is an injury I do not deserve. What I deserve I accept. What I do not deserve pressed on me to humiliate me makes Murder in me. Regardless of the other one -

- it would be simpler and finer for me to do that Murder than to keep it in me. So many times in a week the trembling smothering longing to do that Murder beats, beats in my thin breast. To be so owned by a thing so small: - it is grief and despair and fury and wild nervous intolerableness. It strains my flesh - it wrenches my pulse - it blinds my eyes - it fills my throat -

- it would be a simpler and finer thing to do any Murder than to feel, even once, the strangling damnedness, rising, rising at my throat -

*

Loose Twos

To-morrow

I take it for granted God knows all about me.

If God should read this it would not be news to him.

But his knowledge of me is not immediate knowledge, nor immediately interesting to him. He knows my Twos-and-Twos but he does not make Fours of them.

I am formed of loose Twos which wait for God to make them Fours.

I can not do it myself. When I've tried the added Twos come out threes, seventies, nines, twelves - all the mysterious numbers. Never Fours.

Long ago I decided not to try but to wait for God.

I juggle with temperamental and psychic Twos and experiment in hysteric additions.

But it's no good my trying to make Fours.

If God does not take it up I shall be eternal Twos.

And I seem not greatly to care: whenever that comes home to me I merely light a carefree cigarette.

*

Knitting or Plaiting Straw

To-morrow

The things I know are jumbled and tangled into an indescribable heap inside me.

The things I Don't Know are separated and ranged of their own volition in long orderly rows in my conscious mentality.

The things I know glow with tints and gleams and will-o'-wisp lights and primal colors and waveringly with the blinding gold-purple lightnings of all-Time.

The things I Don't Know glow - each one separately - with a small precise lantern-brightness of its own.

Also in my wide background are things I don't know and am unaware of it: the mass of my luminous Ignorance - it shines with an earthy phosphorescence.

When I look at the things I know I get an undetailed perspective of me like a bird's-eye view of London.

When I look at neat formal rows of things I Don't Know I have a clear look, as if through an uncurtained window into a bare little room, at my quietest self sitting knitting or plaiting straw.

I reckon up and count up and check up lists of big and little things I Don't Know - like this, rapidly: I Don't Know what ink is made of, nor how to fire a Maxim gun: I don't know how to make a will: I don't know how to cook a prairie-chicken, nor what to feed a pet weasel, nor who invented the snarling-iron, nor what it is.

I Don't Know what food people eat in the Himalaya Mountains, nor how Lord Cornwallis felt when he surrendered: I don't know the color of a chicken's gizzard, nor of sand, nor of fish-scales, nor of mice: I don't know whether an English cabinet minister needs strength of mind or strength of will, or both, or neither.

I Don't Know how I hurt the true heart of my friend: I don't know astronomy nor solid geometry: I don't know what I think with: I don't know what ooze leather is, nor who pitched for the Tigers in nineteen-nine.

I Don't Know a good horse from a bad horse: I don't know why a bat sleeps head downward, nor what wasps live on: I don't know how to open oysters, nor how to milk a cow: I don't know the Latin for "whiskey."

I Don't Know whether friendship is a selfish or an unselfish thing, nor who discovered the medlar apple: I don't know what is a jab, fistically speaking, nor a punch, nor a hook, nor a wallop, nor the fighting weight of Packey McFarland: I don't know whether a moth "marries" or whether her eggs are impregnated like a fish's: I don't know why a clasp knife is called a jack knife, nor what to do for an aching foot.

I Don't Know how glass is blown: I don't know whether coal is vegetable or mineral: I don't know the chemical composition of the sunset vapors, nor how to play euchre: I don't know how many guns an armored cruiser carries, nor whether a gorilla meditates: I don't know whether I hate or greatly admire Catherine and Marie de Medici: I don't know a winch from a windlass.

I Don't Know where is the cinnamon bear's native haunt: I don't know how flint is mined, nor if wire is made of steel: I don't know who was the better man - William Wordsworth or the Duke of Wellington: I don't know the advantages of tariff revision downward: I don't know where ex-President Taft will go when he dies.

I Don't Know whether I feel more comfortable with or without my stays: I don't know the origin of the word "dogged": I don't know whether a "full house" is better than "two pairs," nor whether a right merry heart to-day is better than a wrong contented mind to-morrow: I don't know whether rabbit-pie is made of cats in Paris, nor how many sails has a sloop: I don't know what makes a dead body rot.

I Don't Know how to sharpen a carving knife, nor how to roll a cigarette: I don't know the real English meaning of the French noun "élancement": I don't know whether my sex is a matter of my genital organs or of my mental inwards: I don't know how to determine the contents of a circle in square inches, nor how to pronounce "zebra."

I Don't Know whether Edgar Allan Poe is big or little: I don't know how many soldiers fell at Shiloh: I don't know whether temperament or nature or circumstance makes one woman a happy kindhearted whore and another an unhappy cruel-hearted nun: I don't know how to grow artichokes: I don't know what brimstone is, nor how to play the accordion: I don't know what quality in me forms my handwriting.

I Don't Know what-like was my Soul in the Stone Age: I don't know whether cheese is good or bad for my health: I don't know what becomes of discarded hairpins, nor a tooth-brush's ultimate destiny: I don't know the *Fra Diavolo* opera, nor whether anyone ever uses the word "thwack."

I Don't Know whether my heart breaks from within or without: I don't know whether "good old Marie Lloyd" of the London "halls" has a brain like G.K. Chesterton or a dexterous individuality like a juggler: I don't know whether I feel spiritual bliss in my knees or in my spirit: I don't know why I breathe and go on breathing.

I Don't Know what became of the ten lost tribes of Israel: I don't know how to say how-do-you-do to a king: I don't know the exact meaning of my terror and despair: I don't know why I love - why I ever love -

I Don't Know whether laws of chance govern a spinning roulette wheel and ivory ball or whether chance is beyond law: I don't know what kind of missile a Krupp gun shoots: I don't know how a ground-and-lofty tumbler turns a triple-air-summersault: I don't know whether I really am the way I look in the mirror: I don't know whether the Russian language has Romanic roots: I don't know what is the wild power in poetry.

I Don't Know whether lust is a human coarseness or a human fineness: I don't know why death holds a so sweet lure since it would take away my Body: I don't know that I wouldn't deny my Christ, if I had one, three times before a given cockcrow: I don't know on the other hand that I would: I don't know whether honor is a reality in human beings or a pose: I don't know that I mayn't be able to think with my Body when it is in its coffin.

I Don't Know what makes each day a Day of dark Gold and life mournfully precious: I don't know where is God: I don't know how they make tea in Ireland: I don't know how to pronounce the word "girl": I don't know how to make lace: I don't know whether I hear a sound or feel it, nor why a spool of thread looks exactly like a Spool of Thread.

I Don't Know - I Don't Know - I Don't Know, rapidly, to the end of the mystic common-place infinitudes.

- those give me a clear look, as if through an uncurtained window into a bare little room, at my quietest self sitting knitting or plaiting straw -

*

A Life-Long Lonely Road

To-morrow

Fleeting times I wonder if it is my defect or others' that no human family tie holds and warms me.

There is none. I think about it with wistfulness.

The only tie-of-blood feeling that clings to me is of my warming and keeping-alive. And it is very feeble. It grows more feeble.

It is a trivial matter as I look at it universally.

But as I look at it earthlily: there would be an abnormalness, a lostness in one when the mother who bore her got from it at best but a small cool dislike.

It makes me feel humanly lost.

"Lost" is the shuddering life-long lonely word that brushes against me some nights and noons.

*

Their Voices

To-morrow

Every day at half-past ten and half-past two I hear the high shrill sweet choric Voices of hundreds of children shaking the thin clear air.

A public school is but a block from here. The children rush out of it, a hilarious noisy crowd, for a few mid-morning and mid-afternoon minutes. So those minutes, from hearing their Voices day after day, and day after day, have become lyric to my inner-listening.

Their Voices stir me, rouse me, speak to me with old very joyous, very woful meanings.

The children fairly leap out of the school-building through doors and down fire-escape stairways. And their Voices are at once hurled skyward, clamorous and chaotic.

The Sound they make is a roundly common sound yet "winged." It is an untrammeled Sound, uncultivated, only a little civilized.

It is world-music.

In it is the note beyond culture, higher than civilization, and older. It is brave as voices of the shrilling winds and warmer, viriler. It is liltinger than bird-songs and lustier than roarings of mountain cataracts.

Music of the world! -

A little door inside me opens to those Voices.

My little door opens at the first shriek of the first child out of doors, and I hear not only the hundreds of vivid piercing Voices but more - their far-off echoes.

They are the Voices of children, children light-held in crude cold innocence. The eyes of the children are clear - their impulses and instincts rule their little lives. They are yet untouched by the tiredness and terror and shame and sorrow of being human beings.

So the Sound of their Voices sweeps out resistless and regardless as the sea or the sun which makes nothing of its own strength or weakness. And through my little spirit-door I hear them, the poignant common little sweet Voices, echoing, flying away, farther and farther: along the roads: over plains and hills: through valleys long worldly distances from here: through streets: through stone buildings and dingy courts: through big rich houses: through homes of comfort and homes of misery and homes of desolate smugness: into lifeless social foyers: into learned places: into law-courts and cabinet-rooms of nations: into graveyards and churches and down into dead-vaults: into theatres: into clinics: into shops: into factories: into dives and stews and brothels and at lustful doorsteps: into hotels and on sport-courses: into market-places and across battle-fields, round monuments, and in towers and in forts and in prisons and in dungeons: - there along fly their Voices.

It is a brave, brave Sound, and an insistent: nothing stops it.

It is triumph.

The noise of the noisiest battle dies away in time. The pounding of ocean-surf on the rocks and of electric thunder in the clouds are lasting only with this earth. But brave wild Voices of children fly on and on, outlasting a million earths, silencing aeons of thunder, floating strongly back of the stars. The voices of men - wizards, monks, artisans, thieves - echo no farther than their talking conceits: even of poets except as they catch up into their sonance something to interpret a cool gay clamor of child-Voices. The voices of women - singing women, lovely women, angelic honest women - die with their bodies: even of mothers of the children except as they follow with their own echo, by dream and shadow, the thronging child-Voices as they go.

For the Sound of the child-Voices is more potent than wizards' - it is not cramped into thought-forms: more devotional than monks' because super-conscious; more menacing than thieves' because absolute. And it echoes, echoes, echoes in the market-place full-tongued, ringing, rising like the northern gale when all the other voices are long dead-silenced: and after.

Music of the world.

This moment I hear it for it is half-after two of a bright gold day. The air is emotional, nectareal, and mellow and yellow and hot-sparkling. The Voices pierce it like a storm of fine steel arrows. I at once set open my spirit-door and through it come the sweet shrill chorus and the marvel echo beginning and swelling and starting away. It wakes vision so that I see - quick, evil, terribly human, in the dazzlingest daytime colors - all those Places where the Voices go.

I go to a window and watch the children running about beneath the high tide of their Voices. And they and the school-building and the streets and stone walls show in duller colors than the Places where their Echo goes.

- *small girls with clipped hair and bloused cotton frocks, taller girls throwing a basket-ball, thin-legged little girls playing hop-scotch, groups of varied sizes with rainbow ribbons in their hair, confused masses of knitted sweaters and fat white-stockinged legs and shiny leather belts and ankle-strapped shoes, and little young shoulders and knees and waistlines - restless and kaleidoscopic -*

- *and confused boy-groups - little fellows in suits misnamed Oliver-Twist, larger boys of serge-Norfolk persuasion, types of the generic knickerbocker at once motley and monotonous - all with the strong sturdy calves of their legs clad in a time-honored kind of black ribbed stockings, all with the same breed of ties and collars and short-cropped hair, all with the tacit air of confessing themselves the most serenely cruel of all animals -*

A careless conscienceless happy mob.

It is the Sound of their Voices that invests them with the terrifying Power, the long world-sweeping Force as of spirit and matter merged, the human radioactivity not evil and not good, stronger than all evil and all good.

Those children I look at must cease to be children, and must lose their Voices and grow into monks and thieves and singing women - must turn into persons - "Romans, countrymen, and lovers."

But will come after those another chorus: the same chorus: the same Voices.

The brief yellow mellow minutes have passed and the last shout has been silenced and the hundreds of children, Rainbow Hair-Ribbons and Black Ribbed Legs, are again gathered into the McKinley School.

And my little door is shut again: that door opens but for those Voices.

The Voices: their echo flying everywhere flies here into my still room: and it stirs me, rouses me, speaks to me with the old joyous woe.

Music of the world.

*

My Damns

To-morrow

I bear the detailed infliction of being a person with a tired mixture of patience and indifference and scorn.

I say on Monday, Damn the ache in my left foot: on Tuesday, Damn that rattling window - I hate it: on Wednesday, Damn this yellow garter - it's too tight: on Thursday, Damn my futile life: on Friday, Damn the solitude: on Saturday, Damn these thoughts: on Sunday, Damn my two dresses.

But I pronounce each day's Damn in a half-perfunctory half-preoccupied tone, more from duty and fitness than from conviction. I intently mean each Damn, but the scornful indifferent patience which is my spirit-essence leavens each one. I swear at my life's perversities with only a fatigued contempt due partly to bodily fragileness but mostly to a cold continently reckless mood which is clasped on me like a strong stupefied devil-fish. In this mood I should murmur the same gelded Damn if I found myself penniless and foodless in strange streets: if I became suddenly deaf: if my Body were being lashed with whips or raped by a Mexican bandit. I should murmur the same worn Damn if I were this moment on a gallows with the rope around my neck and life were dearly madly precious.

I mark that with my musing regrets. I remember in the strong young furies of eighteen each new day of my life was filled with passionate poetic blasphemy, protests, and rebellions of youth. Those were not tired, not acquiescent, not indifferent to slings-and-arrows, but fiery-blooded quick-pulsed breathless brave young Damns.

There is splendor in being brave in a fighting attitude, but in being brave through indifference there is no splendor.

But it is only toward calamity and adversity and worldly untowardness that I feel indifferent. Fighting blood is stirred in me if not against the hated things then for the loved things. I could fight and I could die, and love it, to save poet-lusters, poet-fineness, poet-beauty from the world's flat griefs. In that, which I feel warm and real and sparkling in my blood, is some splendor for me.

- and also I could die for my country: and there is fighting hatred stirred in me against its foes -

But in poetry there is nothing that evokes a lusty curse against its vulgar adversaries. Poetry floats too high upon its dazzling wings. I get delicately drunk from watching it till I can see the wings' Gold Shadow touch its foes and magically split them into dust-atoms.

So then the morale of my Damns remains perfunctory.

But they are apt and useful. They fit into the nervous rhythms of my life. They mark time in my spirit's flawed action. I begin each day with a Damn of sorts. I end each day with a Damn of sorts. At midday sometimes it's "Damn the terrifying ignorance of people." In the dusk a deep-felt Damn of the blood. In the night another. And at my late eating time a negligible Damn.

A wonderful word, Damn. It means enough and not too much. It means everything in life, and roundly nothing.

Without Damn my day would lack tone. Damn richly justifies each pronouncement of itself in word-value, substance-value, and musical resonance. It harms nobody and it helps me. It destroys nothing and it strengthens me. It damages my annoyances and mends me somewhat.

But - perfunctory, desultory, tiredly, insolent, it would be thrilling to think the hot fire would sometime be back in my Damns. Better that than Youth's faith in my dreams. Better that than the *jeune-fille* beauty in my hair. Better than even Youth's ichor in my veins: Youth's fire in my Damns -

But there is dearness in this mood, which is indifferent and scornful and slightingly patient, though it wants splendor. Let my Damns be always brave, always contemptuous of disaster to me, and they will be first-water value though their kind alter never-so.

*

To God, Care of the Whistling Winds

To-morrow

This morning came a letter from a half-forgot friend in London. She is in vaudeville and has been booked for two months in the Music Halls. Her letter is of a tenor productive of a letter in turn. But I am somehow not free to write letters to friends while I'm living in my two plain dresses. So I wrote this letter to God instead:

19th November

Dear God:

I know you won't answer this letter. I'm not sure you will get it. But I have the feeling to write you a letter, though it should only blow down the whistling winds.

I haven't a thing to ask of you: no prayer to make. I am not suppliant nor humble nor contrite. Nor would I justify myself as a person in your eyes. I scorn to try to justify myself. What I am I am. If I am a bad actor I take the results of it without plaint. I comment on it - why not? - since cats may look at kings and each person inherits four-and-twenty hours a day. But I am bewildered and distraught and sad.

The best you do for me, God, when I think of you - you personally - is to make me bewildered and distraught and sad.

But I've imagined I could put myself to you as a proposition to take or to leave as you like: on my terms since I do not know yours.

There are some verses - the *Rubaiyat* - in which you are upbraided as if you might be the dealer in some gambling game who had the long end of all the wagers and still so protected his money that *he* could not lose however the cards turned. - "from his helpless creature be repaid pure Gold for what he lent him dross-allayed." - "thou who didst with pitfall and with gin beset the Road I was to wander in. -"

But to me that seems a cheap attitude toward you, God. I admit you are fair. If I thought you weren't my mind would not vex itself with you at all. I can not make you out a crooked dealer nor one who lends out bad money and demands good money in repayment.

But you are reticent and cold-tempered and uninterested. So it seems. The necklace which you gave me so long ago, made of little curses, I wear always round my spirit-neck. It serves some purpose, perhaps, and it answers as a keepsake: so at least I may not forget you whether or not you forget me. I don't ask any more of your attention nor anything more of you than I would be willing to give you in return. But I wish you would be willing to exchange attention with me. I am lonely. I am terrified. I am frightfully overshadowed by myself and my odd aloofness and my thronging solitary emotions and my menacing trivialities. I am always fearing not that I may be wicked or immoral or allied with evils - I don't really care a tinker's curse about that - but that I may be growing petty and trivial and weak. It is horrible, horrible to feel that I may be a weakling - you, God, may not know how horrible to me. It is like black annihilation for all eternity when my Soul longs frantically, desperately to live. I feel weakness to be the only immoralness - hateful and vile in whatever aspect. I want to be strong to endure and to live in noonday lights and to overcome my poorness. I want, though I'm far from it, to be brave and big. What I admire you for, though you're so far off and strange and inexplicable, is that you are strong. You are Strength, you are Light, you are the Solution and the Absolute. You'd hardly know what weakness is if it did not so crop out in this human race you made. This human race is a faërily beautiful thing: star-flaming poets have sung in it: lovely youth has breathed upon it: happy wild hearts have informed it. But the odd keynote of it all is weakness. And I have felt me tuned overmuch by that keynote.

- but I won't be weak, I won't be, I won't be, God! Whether you pay attention or not, whether I breathe only futileness, I will be strong, strong, strong in myself - strong if only in my falseness - strong and strong again -

This would be your chance with me if you cared to take it: because I own now just my plain two dresses. When I grow out of this quiet mood - (if ever I do: I begin to doubt it) - I shall have more dresses, and then I shall think about them, God, and the phases of life they'll build up around me, and not about you. It's not that pretty frocks would take my attention away from you if you once claimed it. Once you claimed my attention it would be yours forever. But pretty frocks would mean I am again walking in paved peopled roads. Being there without your attention I shall go where my garments may lead me forgetful of you. One's life is of the flavor of one's clothes: "the wine must taste of its own grapes."

Now feels like a fitting time for you to be personal with me, to give me a sign that you know I'm here. I know I am blind and ignorant about that. You may know a time that shall be more fitting, a time when my still mood and two dresses are long gone and my life is made of fluff and lightness so your sign will crash into it like a black two-ton meteor.

I only tell you how it seems. If you should come now and speak to me I should feel suddenly glad. To-day feels such a day-of-God. The sky is all wet silver and the air a thin cloud of gold. I sit writing you by my window, often looking out with my forehead resting against the cool pane. There is an ache in my forehead, in my insteps, in my backbone, and in my spirit. By stopping in here a moment you would gladden me. If you could give me, or show me - where it perhaps had always been - one true thing to have always in my life I should cling to it and ask nothing of it but that it remain true. If you'd make me one far-off promise of a dawn to come after this tired darkness I would take your word for it and would walk toward your dawn in a straight road from which I should not ever turn aside. In me is a small torch glowing though set in chaos. By its light I should keep in the road leading to your dawn. I should keep in it at any sacrifice to my merely human self: any sacrifice, believe me.

It isn't a bargain I would make with you. I don't like the thought of a bargain with you. I would rather take the chance and lose honestly: not in everything but in this matter with you. You show me the road and I take it for the sole reason that it's a true one. I should expect myself to pay the tolls - heavy ones since I'm innately a liar, a someway bad lot. I know, the same as I know one and one make two, that I've only to be square in the human business of living to get back a square deal, though I'll get badly battered, with it. But it isn't what I mean. Something inside me hungers for answeringness - a Gleam - to make me know the worldly squareness and the battering are worth while beyond themselves: but a detail in the game.

You mightn't guess it but I am diffident about broaching this much that may sound like a plea, so I'll say no more of it.

But before I close the letter I want to tell you that I'm not wanting in gratitude for the terrible beauty of this world. I feel with ecstasy the burning loveliness of the life you give the human race.

I want to tell you thank-you for some things in it. But all that they mean I can not tell in words.

Only yesterday a light at sundown lingered on the hill-tops and on the desert back of the School of Mines in tints of Olive and Copper and Ochre and Rose so delicate, so radiant, so dumbly forlorn that I closed my eyes against it all as I walked along the sand: its aliveness, its realness, its flawless golden dreadful peace tortured and twisted and too-keenly interpreted me.

And one summer-day in Central Park in New York I saw a little Yellow-Yellow Butterfly fluttering above a small plot of brilliant Green-Green Grass in the afternoon sunshine. To you, God, used to the purpling splendor of untold worlds that mightn't seem noteworthy. But to me - because I am half-sister to so many trivialities the Yellow-Yellow of those little wings and the sweet bright Green of the clipped velvet Grass beneath the sun suddenly fiercely entered in and beat-beat hard on my imagination. O the glare and the flare of that fairy prettiness! I shall never forget that picture though I should one day see those worlds. It made me think wildly of you, God, at the time - and ever since. It is there yet in Central Park, that particular plot of Grass, and if not that Yellow-Yellow Butterfly - happily, happily Yellow it was - then another!

And to-day and often other days I read this -

Heard melodies are sweet, but those unheard are sweeter -

- magic words: potent hushed wizardry of beauty.

It opens the doors of all the Inner Rooms and more blest, more precious, of the celestial brain of him who wrote it. In making the glimmering Purple of all your worlds, God, you have not surpassed the thing you made in the regal wistful glory of John Keats.

And two nights ago I went close to my glass and looked deep into my own dark gray eyes, and they were beautiful. Their color is the gray not of peace but of stormy sky and clouded sea. Their expression is alien and melancholy and they are never without circlings of fatigue or stress. And when I meet their glance they mostly accuse and condemn and confound me. But two nights ago they grew wide and deep and breathless-looking at realizing me human and alive. And presently I saw, back of their gray iris - my Soul: like a naked girl: like a willow in the wind: like a drowning star at daybreak: an inherent inexpressible grace - my Soul of many ages.

And this moment another little memory, God, of a tropic marsh a little way back from the sea on the island in the bay at St. Augustine, as it looked in the wane of one sun-flooded February day. In the marsh were tall waving feathery salt-marsh grasses, and little pools of murky water. And there were snail-shells and ancient barnacles and smooth beach pebbles. And bordering the pools were reeds and flags and tiny wax-petaled death-white lilies. By a mound of wet moss was a slim wild blue heron standing on one leg and staring about and preening its blue feathers. And over all the scene was a Pink-Pink Flush. The curving quivering tops of the long grass were Pink with it. The pools were dull Pink mirrors. The barnacles, the pebbles, the death-white lilies were as if a thin bloody veil had been flung down on them. Pink touched the heron's wings, its beak, its head, its glittering beady eyes and spindly leg. The sinking sun shot a Pink broadside of dream-dust all over the marsh: it lingered and hung and floated. Almost I could have reached out my two hands and gathered a bouquet of Pink Flush. The stillness, which was intense, was Pink stillness. O but it was pleasant, pleasant, pleasant, God - it wrapped me in a scarf of Pink sweetness: it filled my throat with Pink honey: it laid on me a gentle eager quiet covetous Pink spell.

Nobody knows how you do it, God. But it is all - Sunset Tint, Yellow-Yellow Moth, Conscious Soul, Poet-Flame - maddening and precious and terrifying and transfiguring to me who live among it. I cherish it as a lonely one may who loves it with passion and is never happy in it. And for it all I thank you, God.

Yours very sincerely,
Mary MacLane

I wrote the Letter on my long-unused monogram note-paper to please my whim, and put it in the envelope and addressed it to God, care of the Whistling Winds. He may receive it - what do I know - only *he* knows, and is reticent.

I only know he'll not answer it.

*

A Working Diaphragm

To-morrow

I am not Respectable nor Refined nor in Good Taste.

I take a delicate M.-Mac-Lane pleasure in those facts.

I doubt if they are anyway peculiar to me, but they feel like a someway delicious clandestine circumstance: something to enjoy all to myself.

It is difficult to imagine any woman really Respectable on her inner side, the side that is turned toward herself alone. And it's certain no woman is Refined: it feels not possible. (There are yet inland places where the word is used in its smug sense and believed in.) And no woman but a dead woman in her coffin is in complete Good Taste. Every live woman has for instance a working diaphragm: and in a diaphragm there is, in the final analysis, simply no taste at all.

(As for men - except poets - I mean *poets*: and perhaps scientists - they are so ungenuine: a race of discreet cautious puppets: wooden dolls who move as their strings are pulled: with nothing so real about them inside as even outside - what use to dwell upon them?)

Nearly all women are perplexingly interesting as human beings. And I am quite the most interesting human being I know: and with it the most appealing, the most sincere - in my own false fashion, and the most bespeaking.

It is much due to knowing and feeling me to be not Respectable nor Refined nor in Good Taste: particularly to being not in Good Taste.

One autumn evening in Boston I went to dine with a man in his apartment in Beacon Street. He is a mining engineer whom I have known since we were both children. He had bidden me to dinner in his off-hand engineering way, but when I arrived at his diggings he was not there. He did not come. Instead there was a dinner waiting, a Japanese boy to serve it, and a strange man who had happened in. The strange man had iron-gray hair, a brow like Apollo, a jowl like Bill Sikes, and much conversation. He said that he was newly from China, South Africa, and Egypt and that in his life he had been married seven times with book and bell. Together we ate the dinner, talking pleasantly in the light of colored Chinese lamp-shades. There were little birds to eat and Chinese wine to drink - *sam shu* distilled virilely from rice: always a little of it is too much. After the dinner we were standing by a teakwood sideboard and the strange man was holding me tightly in his arms against a large smooth evening panel of shirt-front, and he was kissing my mouth with a great deal of ardor. I did not like it. I thought of all the women he had married and wondered if they had liked it. And I mused in my placid brain, "As I was going to St. Ives I met a man with seven wives." It was the only thought in my mind as I waited boredly for him to have done. (It's no good struggling.) And that incident I know was not Respectable.

And one summer day I was riding horseback up a steep gorge in these Montana hills. It was hot dusty riding. I came to a mountain stream with a beautiful little white-and-blue cascade tumbling over a high rock upon smooth pebbles below. I got down from my horse, took off my dusty khaki suit and all my clothes and stood under the fall of the little tumbling cascade, whitely naked, without so much as a figleaf's covering. It was delectable and pagan, what with my quaint thoughts as I stood crouched beneath the sparkling splash. And I know there was nothing Refined in it.

And one evening between nine and ten, a week ago. I was walking across the broad desert valley east of this Butte. It is late November and the night was stormy. A strong high gale swept the Flat. Presently it rained. I was on my way back with a mile or two to go. It rained harder. Heavy sheets of black water whipped and whirled down on me and wrapped me in their wet wings. I love all weather when it is mild and more when it is rough except when it bears down too hard: then I feel indifferent to it. As I moved along the dark road not hurrying and not loitering I was saying inside me, "Why am I going to any shelter out of this heavy wet rain? Why am I not a houseless beggar-woman with nothing gentler in all my life than this November storm? It is not because I deserve gentler things -" And with a sudden heavy shudder I whispered, "I wish I were a beggar-woman! I wish I had no roof to cover me in this cold night-blackness. It would be honest: I should be stripped to my deserts. And I wish it were so - this drenching rain, this strangling wind - nothing but this - shelter, money, comfort, self-satisfaction, however seemingly earned, are dishonest - thieved. I ought to be - ragged beggar - bleared eyes - dirty petticoats - a foul ratty hole to creep into - hunger - bodily misery - all the portion of outcasts - As God may hear me - I'd eagerly tremblingly change lives this moment with a beggar-woman. I would - I would! -" It is a piece of clear inside truth about myself. And I know it proves me to be in poor Taste.

It is a matter of attitude. Each of those incidents might happen to any woman - except perhaps the last. I have known but one girl who agreed with me in such a feeling. And not quite that feeling. She had married a lot of money with a horrible old gentleman and had wearied of both. But the other two episodes could readily belong to any woman of *esprit* who might be on the outside both respectable and Refined: even a woman lawyer.

But my attitude in the incident of the strange iron-gray man, though in a bored way I could have viciously knifed him, was not a Respectable attitude. I was bored and fanciful when doubtless I ought to have been breathlessly angry. But my breathless anger is too rare and beautiful an emotion to waste on ridiculous strange iron-gray men. In the incident of the sparkling cascade my attitude was shameless: something of the sort. It is never reprehensible for a woman to take a cold shower-bath in solitude and health. But my spirit rose and rejoiced at my bodily nakedness and then grew nymph-like and figleafless on its own account. My sex exploited itself in mental visions, like of Leda and the Swan or of myself as a slim villainous Scotch Aphrodite conceived by a bold surprising Titian. And doubtless I ought to have felt timorous in the vast sunlit mountainside, or like a sexless child (or merely "hygienic" like William Muldoon and Bernarr McFadden). But the quick charm of the situation and the heavenly anguish of the icy water, and my lovely Body, and my odd moralless musings were too intriguing to expend themselves banalely.

The wet night road and the beggar-woman wish: it is drearily real to me. Though I wear two plain dainty dresses, in a house - in me, beating, beating, pounding down is a cold wild heavy rain: and under my feet a long lonely muddy road. If they belong to me - well. I love Me the more for feeling them.

And I feel them because I am not yet dead and in my coffin, but alive and with a working diaphragm: which diaphragms are in not Good Taste.

*

Lot's Wife

To-morrow

To-day in the afternoon I briskly manicured my fingernails, sitting by my gold-and-blue window, and I mused upon Lot's Wife.

So many persons and incidents and events and adventures and episodes there are to muse upon, in this mixed world, dating from when it began till now. There's something to charm any mood. Let me leave the doors of my mind open and anything at all may float in like an errant butterfly on a summer's day.

It is an entertaining world, by and large: a limitless vaudeville.

Lot's Wife is to me a fantasy from the antique, a bit of archaic frivol to beguile me.

When first I heard of her, from an acrid aunt of caustic humor who told me the tale tersely in explanation of a biblical print, I was seven years old. From that day to this my meditative thoughts have from time to time flitted backward to dwell interestedly upon Lot's Wife. Later when I went to an Episcopal Sunday-school I was pleased to find this adjuration in according-to-St-Luke: "Remember Lot's Wife." There seemed no special meaning attached to it. It seemed like Remember Lot's Wife in any way you like - as it might be with a card on her birthday, a useless gift at Christmas, in your prayers, or in retributive patriotism like Remember the Alamo, Remember the Maine.

But I remember her because I like her.

There's no name given for Lot's Wife in the brief biblical narrative, so I long ago named her Bella as expressive of the temperament and character that have grown around her image in my thoughts.

Poor Bella, I ruminated as I tinted and polished my nails. Her life in Sodom was not entirely satisfying to her. Sodom was a town completely given over to pleasure of the physical and outward sorts. The dwellers lived in and for their physical senses alone. And Bella had it in her to care for the foods of the spirit. Not that she longed for them - she was not so conscious of herself - but she had it in her to care for them had they been given her. Still, Sodom and its ways were the best she knew and she had known them all her life. The roots of her temperament had shot down into the Sodomesque substrata. She fondly loved the place.

Sodom was a prototype for Babylon or Pompeii, worshiping the hotness of the sun in moralless plaisance, with fetes and drinkings of wine from gold and silver cups, and bathings in warm scented marble-lined pools, and anointings with oils of olive and palm, and dwellings among flowers of thin bright petals and birds of vivid plumage and fountains of crystal and rainbow, and caterings to the sparkle and froth of human emotions, and browsings amid loves and lights o' love. Can Bella be wondered at for growing fond of it all, having known nothing substantialer? And can she rightly be blamed for hating the thought of leaving it for dry sage-brush wilds in the mountains? She did hate and dread that thought with all her soul from the moment it was made known to her that Sodom for its sins was booked for destruction. She had perhaps a fortnight in which to dread it, and a fortnight if given over to dread is long enough to damage stronger spirits than hers.

Bella was slender and svelte, with long straight soft beautiful silken pale red hair and white-lidded eyes of grayish green. She was thirty-eight - a young thirty-eight. There's an old thirty-eight which applies to greedy school teachers, gangrenous woman government-clerks, fading hard-hearted stenographers, over-righteous woman doctors; to all whose virtue is ever indecently on guard. But there's a glory-tinted sun-kissed young thirty-eight which applies to sensitive high-strung generously-emotional women like Bella Lot. She had smooth hands with supple tapering fingers, an irregular expressive-lipped mouth like a pimpernel-bloom, firm slim feet, and the quivering suggestive white knees of a wood-nymph. From any angle-of-view can she be blamed for hating to take that equipment away from the city-de-luxe which was its so proper setting and hiding it in the sage-brush?

Furthermore Bella had a lover in Sodom. It is beyond a sane effort of the imagination that she could have loved that unpleasing old man Lot. The best and worst that can be said of him is that he was a fit addition to the company of the old Patriarchs who were for the most part an exceeding craven crew. The martyrs, the sages, and especially the prophets had their splendors. But the lean old patriarchs - The sporting blood of all of them, in the sense of merest simplest courage - from Adam down, would hardly aggregate one drop. There are any number of reasons - as many as Bella had charms - to account for Lot's having married her. But what she could have seen in him to make her wish or even willing to be married to him is a deep mystery to me. It may have been his family. I believe Bella lacked family: she was just a person. And was he not nephew to Abraham? But even being niece-in-law to Abraham himself seems insufficient compensation for being Lot's Wife.

The Lots had two young daughters, one fifteen and one seventeen, it might be. I do not know their names - call them Ethel and Agnes. But they were of a recalcitrant temper and absorbed in their own racy pastimes among the younger youth of Sodom and they had no need of their mother. Besides, they "took after" their father. So Bella was fain to turn outward in search of nurturing matter whereon to feed her humanness. Had it been expected of her to play fair with the patriarch she would have played fair. But it was not expected of her by anyone in Sodom - far from it, and least of all by the patriarch. She was eight-and-thirty, and Lot - *he* was doubtless eight or nine hundred years old, after the surprising long-lived fashion of the period.

So Bella found a lover ready and awaiting her. She would have found a lover in the circumstances even without caring to. But she quite cared to, I think. Everything points that way, and when one remembers that good old man her husband one can not censure her but only pity her. Be it as it may she had one - one as real as anything could be in that town of sparkling froth.

Of the lover's identity - little is known, as the historians say. My fancy as I filed my fingernails failed me on the point. Suffice it to state that ever and anon as time passed in Sodom the gray-green eyes of Bella were gazed into with fondness, affection, adoration, and desire: the white eyelids of Bella had showers of light kisses bestowed on them, soft-falling as rose-petals shaken loose in summer winds: the tapering white hands of Bella were caressed and caressing with the oddly intense tenderness of physical love: the pale red hair of Bella was ruffled and fluffed and disarrayed by the fingers of love: the red-pimpernel mouth of Bella was touched, bruised, clung to by the lips of love: the svelte whiteness and nymph-knees of Bella glowed as she broached love's arms: - and all went much merrier than marriage bells. In short, Bella paid herself with usury for the deadliness of being Lot's Wife.

And there we have the crux of Bella's dread of leaving Sodom and its tempered sweetness for the arid sage-brush hills and the respectively cold and hectic companionship of the good old patriarch and the recalcitrant daughters.

It can not be claimed for Bella that any white poetic fires gleamed across her soul, that any limning beauty shone palely from within her. The air of Sodom was not conducive to suchlike matters and Bella was no finer than her breeding and generation. But she was gentle and wistful and kind of heart. She was lovely to look at and ingenuously lovable in her clinging affection and disarming naturalness. She was all one could want to imagine in the word "charming."

Came the night set for destruction and the Lot family fled according to schedule. They fled away in the early damps of an autumn evening through the outer city gates and along a rough road faintly lit by a dying moon. They had three separate reasons for fleeing. Lot fled because he was a patriarch and was given to doing craven Old-Testamentish things of that sort: Bella fled because she was Lot's Wife and obliged to act out the role: and Ethel and Agnes fled because they had true patriarchal blood in their veins and had therefore no marked inclination to remain in Sodom to be annihilated - "safety first" was one of their watchwords. They fled in the van. Lot came after them, being less swift of foot. Bella lagged behind. She didn't want to go. Every way she looked at it she didn't want to go. She hated that flight for a thousand reasons.

The ghastly moon shed a terror on her with its dim rays. The ground was hard and rutted with frosty mud and bruised her slender feet through her white buckskin sandals.

She wore a loose *ninon* gown of white silk and linen with a gold girdle around her narrow loins and a gold clasp at the left shoulder. Binding her long hair, so palely red in the moon, was a white-and-gold fillet. In one hand she carried a gold-and-enamel link bracelet, a gift but that afternoon from the lover. Suddenly she stopped and cried to herself, "I'm too lovely for this fate - I'm too lovely and beloved - the cruelty of God - : I'll not go on!" She thought of the gleams and colorings of Sodom. She quickly reckoned the cost and decided to pay it. She was a rare good sport, and a quaint. She looked back at the doomed city blazing in brimstone - "But his wife looked back from behind him, and she became a pillar of salt." - As I put away my chamois-skin buffer and glass paste-jar through my mind floated the pensive burden of a by-gone French song -

Oh, the poor, oh, the poor, oh, the poor - dear - girl -

She must have made a beautiful statue, all in glistening salt.

I wish I had a glistening little salty replica of it to set on my desk: a so unusual, a so dainty conceit, Lot's Wife!

*

My Echoing Footsteps

To-morrow
While I live so still in this life-space, while I muse and meditate and analyze everything I touch, while I walk, while I work, while I change from one plain frock to the other: in quiet hours roiled tumbling storms of vicarious unhopeful Passion whirl, whirl in me: Passion of Soul, Passion of Mind, Passion of living, Passion of this mixed world: in terror, in wild unease, in reasonless mournful joy.

I never knew real Passion, Passion-meanings, till I reached thirty. It's now I'm at life's storm-center, youth's climax, the high-pulsed orgasmic moment of being alive.

At twenty the woman chrysalid soul and aching pulses awaken in crude chaste Spring-cold beauty. At forty her fires either have subsided to dim-glowing coals or leaped to too-positive, too-searing, too-obvious flames

- her bones and the filigrees of her spirit may be alike dry, brittle-ish. But at thirty her Spring has but changed to midsummer. Poesy still waits upon her Passions.

My spring has changed, bloomed, burst to midsummer.

Soft electrical heat-currents of being swing and sweep around me. They touch me and enter my veins. But the liquid essences of youth still quell and compress them. I am at youth's climax - a half-sullen, half-smouldering youth which still is youth.

My rose of life is fragrant and aglow. Its sweet pink petals are uncurled and conscious in the wavering light.

Winds flutter and stir and rumple and twist those petals -

To-day is a To-morrow of countless unrests. Large and little Passions beat at me all the blue-and-copper day. I walked my floor with irregular lagging steps. I felt menacing, dangerous to myself, dynamic as nitro-glycerine: and smoothly drearily sane as a bar of white soap. I stood at my window and looked long at the circling range of mountains which skirt this Butte. Nothing else I have looked at, of sea or plain or hill, affected me like that chain of barren peaks. They are arid splendor and pale purple witchery and grief and lasting sadness and deathlike beauty and woe and wonder. Their color quietly stormed my eyes and blurred them with tears.

It was a mood in which any color or gleam or thought or strain of music or note of sad world-laughter or any un-sane loveliness of poetry could enchant or flay or transport me to my frayed last nerve.

There is terror in facing death on battlefields, on sinking ships, in black ice-floes, in blazing buildings. But to me no death, for I fear no death, could be so dreadfully pregnant with in-turning woe and frenzy and all intolerable feeling as facing starkly my futile life.

My life is a vast stone bastile of many little Rooms in which I am a prisoner. I am locked there in solitude on bread and water and let to roam in it at will. And each Room is tenanted by invisible garbled furies and dubious ecstasies. I run with echoing footsteps from Room to Room to escape them: but each Room is more unhabitable than the last. There are scores of little Rooms, each with its ghosts, each different.

In one Room silent voices in the air accuse my tired Spirit of wanton vacillations and barren lack of purpose and utter waste, waste, waste of itself. And they threaten death and destruction. I know that accusation and I hate it: I hate it the more for that it's wholly just. To escape it I run from that Room along a dim passage into another one. In it unseen fingers clutch my Heart. In their touch also is an accusation: of selfishness and waste and want of something to beat for: and in their touch is the savor of wild wishes and human longings and passionate prayers for something warm and simple and real to rest against: and in their pressing clutching turbulent touch is a tormenting half-promise, chance-promise, no-promise: and the hovering inevitable threat of death and destruction. That too I know and hate and half-love: and I can't bear it. So I run out of that Room along a passage and into another. I hear my footsteps echoing as I run.

- as a child when I ran in the early night through a dark leaf-lined tunnel-like driveway the sound of my own flying footsteps on the hardened gravel was the only thing that frightened me. I quite believed there were bears in the brushwood on either side, but fear of them never struck to the core of my child-being like the unknown thing in my echoing steps. And it is fear I feel now from the ghost-sound of my ghost-footsteps running, running away from the little Rooms. It is realer to me now than were my child footsteps to my child-self long ago: it is more definite than my hand which writes this: it is hideous -

Out of a dim passage I run into another little Room. In it some gray filmy threads, like strands of loose cobwebs caught on ceilings, float about. They sweep gently against my cheeks and hands and neck, and cling and twine and lightly hold with the half-felt feeling peculiar to bits of cobwebs on the skin. And it torments my woman-flesh with calefaciant thrills fierce and goading and sweet. There also is the accusation, now against my Body; for tissues and strength wasted: for useless fires meant to warm human seeds to life, meant to make me fruitful, meant to make me bear dear race-burdens: accusation for the cosmic waste of hot objectless desire, for the subtle guilt of a Lesbian tendency, for an unleashed over-positive sex-fancy. With it too is the lowering promise of death and destruction. It also is just. But out of my borne-along helplessness in it comes no culpable emotion because of cobweb thrills and their arraignment but only a wearing wearying despair. I rush out of that Room in shrugging impatience, with only scorn for a threat of death, for a threat of destruction - but with a wild fear of my own flying steps. I hurry and hurry on from door to door: but it's no good. In some other Room my brain is anathematized from frowning walls as an impish demoniac power which I use with no good intent and therefore with bad intent: and again I shrink and run away. In another Room are all the lies I have ever told: I have told legions - my own peculiar lies, gentler on me than truths: they dart around me in the Room like black heavy-winged moths, clouds of them fluttering at my forehead. They drive me out shivering. In another Room four times when I was a not-good-sport confront me in a row like pictures and sting me and make me hide my eyes: I'd rather be a leper, a beast, a maniac than a not-good-sport (for my own precious reasons) - and I rush away again. In some other Room -

- the same galling torment in all the Rooms. Wherever I run with the echo-echo of steps there are Accusing voices and half-formed Prayer and uncertain Yearning and violent yet dumb and inexpectant Protest and the unfailing Threat of death and destruction: not earth-death but universe-death: death and death and death everywhere coming on and on: myself knowing the just note in it all and from it grown numb with some cold and restless terror. Also I know no door I run through with my panic-feet will ever set me free of the bastile except a death door: the earthly death of this tired life -

But it's from this maelstrom that the flashing burning sparkling mad magic of being alive leaps out brilliant and barbarous - and throbbing and splendid and sweet. A merely human hunger comes back on me. Then I want all I ever wanted with a hundredfold more voltage of wanting than I have ever yet known.

I am all unhopeful, all unpeaceful, all a desperate Languor and a tragic Futileness: I am an unspeakably untoward thing.

And already I have been seared and scarred trivially from standing foolishly near some foolish human melting-pots.

No matter for any of it. I want to plunge headlong into life - not just imitation life which is all I've yet known, but honest worldly life at its biggest and humanest and cruelest and damnedest: to be blistered and scorched by it if it be so ordered - so that only it's *realness* - from the outside of my skin to the deeps of my spirit.

It is not happiness I want - nothing like it: its like never existed since this world began.

I want to feel one big hot red bloody Kiss-of-Life placed square and strong on my mouth and shot straight into me to the back wall of my Heart.

I write this book for my own reading.

It is my postulate to myself.

As I read it it makes me clench my teeth savagely: and coldly tranquilly close my eyelids: it makes me love and loathe Me, Soul and bones.

Clench and close as I will the winds flutter and stir and crumple and twist my petals as *they* will: - as I sit here tiredly, tiredly sane.

*

A Comfortably Vicious Person

To-morrow

The blue-and-copper of yesterday is dead and buried this To-morrow in a maroon twilight.

I this moment saw darkly from my window the somber hills in their heavy spell of pale-purple and grief and splendor and sadness and beauty and wonder and woe.

But their color brings no tears to my wicked gray eyes.

The passion-edged mood is burnt out.

Gone, gone, gone.

I listlessly change into the other black dress for listless dinnertime and all my thought is that my abdomen is beautifully flat and that I must purchase a new petticoat.

I rub a little rouge on my pale mouth and I idlingly recall a clever and filthy story I once heard.

I laugh languidly at it and feel myself a comfortably vicious person.

I pronounce a damn on the familiar ache in my beloved left foot and turn away from myself.

I stick out the tip of my forked-feeling tongue at the bastard clock on the stairs. I note the hour on it with a fainness in my spirit-gizzard to dedicate Me from that time forth to a big blue god of Nastiness: Nastiness so restful, humorous, appetizing, reckless, sure-of-itself.

- these hellish To-morrows creeping in their petty pace: they bring in weak-kneed niceness, and they bring in doubts, and they bring in meditation and imagery and all-around humanness, till I'm a mere heavy-heeled dubious complicated jade

*

In My Black Dress and My Still Room

To-morrow

I have fits of Laughter all to myself.

The world is full of funny things. All to myself I Laugh at them. I lounge at my desk in the small night hours, and I finger a pencil or a box or a rubber or a knife and rest my chin on my hand, and sit on my right foot, and Laugh intermittently at this or that.

Ha! ha! ha! I say inwardly: with all my Heart: relishingly.

I laugh at the thought of a mouse I once encountered lying dead - so neat, so virtuous - though soft and o'er-long dead - with its tail folded around it - in a porcelain tea-pot: a strong inimical anomaly to all who viewed it. It had a look of a saint in effigy in a whited sepulcher. Looked at as a mouse it seemed out of place. Looked at as a saint it was perfect.

I Laugh at the recollection of a lady I once met who had thick black furry eyebrows incongruous to her face, which she took off at night and laid on her bureau. They were at once "detached" and detachable: itself a subtle phenomenon. She referred to her mind as her "intellects" and talked with a quaint bogus learnedness, and in remarkable grammar, of the Swedenborgian doctrines. Looked at as a person she was inadequate. Looked at as a conundrum she was gifted and profound.

I Laugh at that extraordinary tailor in the Mother Goose rhyme - him "whose name was Stout," who cut off the petticoats of the little old woman "round about," herself having recklessly fallen asleep on the public highway. The tale leaves me the impression that such were the straitly economic ideas of the tailor that he obtained all his cloth by wandering about with his shears until he happened upon persons slumbering thus publicly and vulnerably. Looked at in any light that tailor is ever surprising, ever original, ever rarely delectable.

I Laugh at William Jennings Bryan.

How William Jennings Bryan may look to the country and world-at-large I have never much considered.

It is all in the angle of view: St. Simeon Stylites may seem rousingly funny to some: Old King Cole may have been a frosty dullard to those who knew him best.

To me William Jennings Bryan means bits of my relishingest brand of gay mournful Laughter.

The ensemble and detail of William Jennings Bryan and his career as a public man, viewed impersonally - as one looks at the moon - are something hectic as hell's-bells.

I remember William Jennings Bryan when his star first rose. It was before Theodore Roosevelt was more than a name: before the battleship *Maine* was sunk at Havana: before Lanky Bob wrested the heavyweight title from Gentleman Jim at Carson: before aeroplanes were and automobiles were more than rare thin-wheeled restless buggies: before the song "My Gal She's a Highborn Lady" had yet waned: before one Carrie Nation had hewn her way to fame with a hatchet. I was a short-skirted little girl devouringly reading and observing everything, and I took note of all those. So I took note of William Jennings Bryan nominated for president by the Democratic convention in eighteen-ninety-six. The zealous Democratic newspapers referred to him, though he was then thirty-six, as the Boy Orator of the Platte. Looked at as a grown man, advocating free coinage of silver at sixteen-to-one, a daring dashing Democrat, he was a plausible thing and even romantic. Looked at as a Boy Orator he turned at once into a bald and aged lad oddly flavored with an essence of Dare-devil Dick, of the boy on the burning deck, of a kind of political Fauntleroy madly matured.

Long years later with the top of his hair and his waistline buried deep in his past he became Secretary of State: and at the same time a Chautauqua Circuit lecturer - entertaining placid satisfied audiences alternately with a troupe of Swiss Yodlers.

Of all things, yodlers. Politics makes strange bedfellows and always did. But never before has the American Department of State combined and vied with the yodler's art to entertain and instruct. Looked at as a monologist he might pass if sufficiently interpolated with ah-le-ee! and ah-le-o-o! Looked at as Secretary of State he is grilling and grueling to the senses: a frightful figure quite surpassing a mouse softly dead in a tea-pot, a pair of detachable fuzzy Swedenborg-addicted eyebrows, a presumptuously economical tailor.

And he entertained the foreign ministers at a state dinner, did this unusual man, and he gave them to drink - what but grape-juice, grape-juice in its virginity. Plain water might have seemed the crystalline expression of a rigid puritanic spirit. Budweiser Beer, bitter and bourgeois, might have been possible though surprising. But grape-juice, served to seasoned Latin Titles and Graybeards and Gold-Braid, long tamely familiar with the Widow Clicquot: that in truth seems, after all the years, boyishly oratorical, wildly and darkly Nebraskan. Looked at as an appetizing wash for a children's white-collared and pink-sashed party, or for anybody on a summer afternoon, grape juice is satisfactory. In the careless hands of William Jennings Bryan with his soul so unscrupulously at peace, the virgin grape juice becomes a vitriolic thing: a defluent purple river crushing one's helpless spirit among its rocks and rapids.

- a terrible American, William Jennings Bryan. He is for "peace at any price." There were some, long and long ago, who suffered and endured one starveling winter in camp at Valley Forge that William Jennings Bryan might wax Nebraskanly fat: and he is valiantly for peace: at any price -

For that my Laughter is tinged with fulfilling hatred.

Rich hot-livered Laughter must have in it essential love or hatred.

To William Jennings Bryan everything he has done in his political career must seem all right.

It is all right, undoubtedly. Just that.

- that Silver-tongued Boy Orator
those Yodlers
that Peerless Leader
that Grape-juice -

They come breaking into my melancholy night-hours with an odd high-seasoned abruptness.

I wonder what God thinks of him.

It might be God thinks well of him.

But I - in my black dress and my still room - I say inwardly and willy-nilly, and with all my Heart and relishingly: Ha! ha! ha!

*

Their Little Shoes

To-morrow

Often in windy autumn nights I lie awake in my shadowy bed and think of the children, the Drab-eyed thousands of children in this America who work in coal mines and factories.

Whenever I'm wakeful and the night is windy and my room is dark and I lie in aloneness - a long aloneness: centuries - then shadows come from far-off world-wildnesses and float and flutter dimly unhappy around my bed. They tell me tales of shame and tame petty hopelessness and trifling despair.

And the one that comes oftenest is the one that tells of those Drab-Eyed children distances from here, but very immediate, who work in coal mines and factories. I read about them in magazines and newspapers, but they aren't then one one-hundredth so real as when their shadow floats as close to me in the windy autumn night.

Once in Pennsylvania I saw a group of children, very Drab in the Eyes and very thin in the necks and legs, who worked in a mill. Their look made its imprint in my memory and more in my flesh. And it comes back as if it were the only thing that mattered as I lie wakeful in the windy night.

The children - unconscious and smiling their small decayed smiles - they are living and being crushed between greed and need as between two murderous millstones. Their frail flesh and their little brittle bones, their voices and their pinched insides, the sweet vague childish looks which belong in their faces are squeezed and crunched by two millstones - squeezed,

squeezed till their scrawny fledgling bodies are dry, breathless, and are gasping, strangling, striving frightfully for life: and still are slowly, all too slowly, dying between two millstones.

If it were their own greed or their own need - but it's the greed of fat people and the need of their own warped gaunt parents. Betwixt the two the children meet homelike hideous ruin. Placidly they are cheated and blighted and blasted, placidly and with the utmost domesticness.

The most darkling-luminous thing about the Drab-Eyed children is that they never weep. They talk among themselves and smile their little dreadful decayed smiles, but they don't weep. When they walk it's with a middle-aged gait: when they eat their noontime food it's as grown people do, with half-conscious economic and gastronomic consideration. They count their Tuesdays and Wednesdays with calculation as work-days, which should be childishly wind-sweptly free. Which is all of less weight than the heavy fact that they never weep.

They reckon themselves fairly fortunate with their bits of silver in yellow envelopes every Saturday. They are permitted to keep a bit of it, each child a bit for herself or himself, so that on Sunday afternoons they lose themselves for precious hours watching Charlie Chaplin. Many pink-faced inconsequent children whose parents nurture them and guard them and eternally misunderstand them are less worldlily lucky. But the pink-faced children often weep - loudly, foolishly like puppies and snarling furry cubs - and wet sweet salt tears of proper childishness are round and bright on their cheeks and lashes. It's a sun-washed blestness for them: they're impelled and allowed to weep. But the Drab Eyes shed no tears - they know no reason why they should. There's no impulse for soft liquid grief in the murderous philosophy of two grinding millstones. And there's no time - the lives of the work-children move on fast. Their very shoes are ground between the millstones.

- their little shoes are heartbreaking. The millstones grind many things along with little-little shoes of children: germs of potent splendid humanness that might grow bigly American in heroic ways or in sane round honesty: germs that might grow into brave barbaric beauty or warm wistful sweetness: germs that would grow into lips blooming tender and fragrant as jonquils or into minds swimming with lyrics: - what is strongly lasting and glorified in the forlorn divine human thing - crumpled - twisted forever when millstones grind children's little poor shoes -

The young Drab Eyes are endlessly betrayed: their very color thieved. There's no reason why they should weep.

But there's a far-blown sound as if ten thousand bad and good worldly eyes were weeping in their stead: with a note in it careless, compassionate, and jadedly menacing.

I seem to hear it in the wakeful windy night. And I hear no world-music pouring out of small throats of work-children shrill with woe-and-joy. The sound they make is a dumb sound, for they never weep: a ghost-wail of partly-dead children borne lowly across this mixed world on a stale hellish breeze.

*

The Sleep of the Dead

To-morrow

When I'm dead I want to Rest awhile in my grave: for I'm Tired, Tired always.

My Soul must go on as it has gone on up to now.

It has a long way to go, and it has come a long way.

My Soul first started on its journey somewhere in Asia before the dawn of this civilization. And it has gone on since through the centuries and through strange phases of Body, terrors of flesh and blood, suffering long. But it has gone someway on, each space of the journey taking it nearer to the journey's-End.

It is the dim-felt memory of those journeys that heaps the Tiredness on me now. Not only is my spirit Tired. Through my spirit my hands are Tired: my knees are Tired: my drooping shoulders: my thin feet: my sensitive backbone. When I lift my hand in the sunshine the weight of the yellow honeyed air bears down and down on it because I'm so Tired. When I start to walk on stone pavements the ache of them is in my feet before I set a foot on them because I'm so Tired. The pulse in my veins Tires my blood as it beats. My low voice, though I speak but rarely - it Tires my throat. My breath Tires my chest. The weight of my hair Tires my forehead and temples. My plain frocks Tire my Body to wear. My swift trenchant thoughts Tire my Mind.

It is not the Tiredness of effort though I strive to the limits of my strength every day.

It is not pain, Restful pain. It is Tired Tiredness.

So when I'm dead I want to Rest awhile in my grave. It *would* Rest me.

In the Episcopal Church they use a ritual of poetic beauty, full of Restful things. One of them is the sleep of the dead. The crucified Nazarene slept three days. But all others of us when we go down into our graves are to sleep until a Judgment Day. "Judgment Day" is preposterous and evilly crude: there's no judgment till each can judge himself simply and cruelly in the morning light. But the sleep of the dead -

- the sleep of the dead. Its sound by itself without the thought is Restful -

And the thought is Restful.

I imagine me wrapped in a shroud of soft thin wool cloth of a pale color, laid in a plain wood coffin: and my eyelids are closed, and my Tired feet are dead feet, and my hands are folded on my breast. And the coffin is nine feet down in the ground and the earth covers it. Upon that some green sod: and above, the ancient blue deep sheltering sky: and the clouds and the winds and the suns and moons, and the days and nights and circling horizons - those above my grave.

And my Body laid at its length, eyes closed, hands folded, down there Resting: my Soul not yet gone but laid beside my Body in the coffin Resting.

- might we lie like that - Resting, Resting, for weeks, months, ages -

Year after long year, Resting.

*

Stickily Mad

To-morrow

It is damn-the-Smell-of-Turpentine!

Here I happen on a damn in me which is not desultory but bloodily strong and alive and alone.

The wood in my blue-white room has been newly painted. For a day and a night I intermittently encounter and go to bed in a spirit of Turpentine. It bears a cruel obscure abortive message to my nerves.

I lie wakeful in the dark and try to reason out a logicalness or poetry in a thing so artfully pestilential.

But I am hysterically lost in it and my heart beats hysterically in it.

I remember the inexpressible ingenuity of man: of white man as against bone-brained savage races. Every invented usefulness feels like divine witch-craft. A pen and a bottle of perfume and a doorknob and a granite kettle and an electric light: I have the use of each since white man is so ingenious. Were I a red Indian I should have only the awkward barbarous stupid tools my race had used a thousand years. I contrast the two as I lie wakeful, with a sense of richness and of detailed repletion and of material blestness.

But at once comes the Smell of Turpentine and announces itself something outside that and *different,* something stronger, something masterfuler than ingenuity and savagery together. It tortures my nerves: it burns my eyes: it lames my flesh: it jerks and flays and garbles my inner body.

The ingenuity of man has produced opium and cocaine which would combat and hide it all behind a heavy curtain of stupor, with effects equally damaging if less grievously subtle.

The Smell of Turpentine is a thing to bear since all its counter-things bring only solider evil.

The paint was put on the wood by a dirty little man whom I briefly inspected as something removed from my range of life. In return he covertly eyed me. I expected my wakeful hours would be punished by strong new paint and be-visioned by dirty little men. But it is all sheer Turpentine with a power suggesting nothing human nor super-natural nor divine. Just itself: a goblin virulence.

In all my Soul and bones and Mary-Mac-Lane-ness it is damn-the-Smell-of-Turpentine as a bastard murderous hurt.

I have an odd feeling God has no more power over it than have I.

It half-calls for a *different* Turpentine God.

I am shakily mad tonight, I believe, from a so slight sticky matter.

*

God Compensates Me

To-morrow

It's a Sunday midnight and I've just eaten a Cold Boiled Potato.

I shall never be able to write one-tenth of my fondness for a Cold Boiled Potato.

A Cold Boiled Potato is always an unpremeditated episode which is its chief charm.

It's nice to happen on a book of poetry on a window-sill. It's nice to surprise a square of chocolate in a glove box.

It's nice to come upon a little yellow apple in ambush. It's nice to get an unexpected letter from Jane Gillmore. It's nice to unearth a reserve fund of silk stockings under a sofa pillow. And especially it's nice to find a Cold Boiled Potato on a pantry shelf at midnight.

I like caviare at luncheon. And I like venison at dinner, dark and bloody and rich. And I like champagne bubbling passionately in a hollow-stemmed glass on New Year's day. And I like terrapin turtle. And I like French-

Canadian game-pie. And artichokes and grapes and baby onions. And none of them has the odd gnome-ish charm of a Cold Boiled Potato at midnight.

I can imagine no circumstance in which a Cold Boiled Potato would not take precedent with me at midnight. If I had a broken arm: if I had a husband lying dead in the next room: if I were facing abrupt worldly disaster: if there were a burglar in the house: if I'd had a dayful of depression: if God and opportunity were knocking and clamoring at my door: I should disregard each and all some minutes at midnight if I had also a Cold Boiled Potato.

I love to read Keats' Nightingale in my hushed life. I love to remember Caruso at the Metropolitan singing Celeste Aïda. I love to watch the bewitching blonde Blanche Sweet in a moving picture. I love to feel the summer moonlight on my eyelids. And it's disarmingly contented I am with a Cold Boiled Potato at midnight.

Content is my rarest emotion and I get it at midnight out of a Cold Boiled Potato.

Some things in life thrill me. Some drive me garbledly mad. Some uplift me. Some debauch me. Some strengthen and enlighten me. Some hurt, hurt, hurt. But I'm not thrilled nor maddened nor uplifted nor debauched nor strengthened nor enlightened nor hurt, but only fed-up and fattened in spirit by a Cold Boiled Potato at midnight.

I stand in the pantry door leaning against the jamb, with a tiny glass salt-shaker in one hand and the sweet dark pink Cold Boiled Potato in the other. And I sprinkle it with salt and I nibble, nibble, nibble. And I say aloud, "Gee, it's good!"

I liked Cold Boiled Potato at four-and-twenty. I liked it at seventeen. I liked it at twelve. At three I climbed on cake-boxes in search of one. And now in the deep bloom of being myself I am made roundly replete at midnight with a Cold Boiled Potato.

A Cold Boiled Potato - it tastes of chestnuts at midnight, the first frost-kissed chestnuts in the woods: and it tastes of rain-water and of salt and of roses: it tastes of young willow-bark and of earth and of grass-stems: it tastes of the sun and the wind and of some nameless relishingness born of the summer hillside that grew it: it tastes at midnight so *like* a Cold Boiled Potato.

A precious peach-colored orchid, an antique spider-web-like lace handkerchief, a delicate purple butterfly, an emerald bracelet: I'd strive for each of those in an eagerly casual way. But it's like an ogre at midnight I pounce on a Cold Boiled Potato.

A Cold Boiled Potato reminds me of the Dickens books in which so much food is eaten cold and tastes so savory - even the "wilderness of cold potatoes" portioned to the Marchioness by Sally Brass. And it reminds me of the Rip Van Winkle play - "give this fellow a cold potato and let him go." And it reminds me of Hamlet - funeral baked meats might include it. And it reminds me of Robin Hood's merry men, and Huckleberry Finn, and the Canterbury Pilgrims, and the Prodigal Son, and all the picturesque wayfarers. It reminds me of the poor as a colorful race wrapped around with hungry romance. It reminds me that life is full of life - rich and fruitful and evolutionary and cosmic: few things feel so cosmic as a Cold Boiled Potato at midnight. It makes me want as I nibble to plant a field of potatoes on a southern-exposed hill and hoe them and dig them all by myself: and give all but one to the poor and Boil that to eat Cold at midnight.

I have to be very hungry to crave a Cold Boiled Potato, but being hungry no possible morsel of food can so interest me at midnight. The same potato hot is domestic and tasteless. The same potato at ten in the evening lukewarm within and sodden with memories of dinner, is a repellent item. At midnight it is all unexpected magnetism.

At midnight my whole being is profoundly courteous, wooingly cordial toward a Cold Boiled Potato.

If I had only what I deserved my portion might well be a Cold Boiled Potato. Intrinsically it is rated low and I know me to be a sort of jezebel. But I'd wonder each midnight if whoever metes out the deserts in this surprising universe knew with what gust I rise at it - *would* I get it.

Nor am I satisfied like the meek and lowly with my midnight supper of Cold Boiled Potato: damn the meek and lowly. It's a satanic delight I take in it. It's a sly private orgie I make of it: a pirate's banquet, a thieves' picnic, a pagan rite, a heathen revelry, a conceit all and unhallowedly my own. My thoughts as I nibble are set mostly on my villainies. No food I eat brings me so broad a license of feeling - a sense of freedom - as a Cold Boiled Potato at midnight.

On a Cold Boiled Potato at midnight I am lightly valorous: call me a trickster and I'll call you a rotter: call me a liar and I'll call you a traitor: call me a coward and I'll call you another: not pugnaciously but gayly and serenely.

I am then in my most bespeaking mood. Anyone who met me standing nibbling in a pantry doorway at midnight would be charmed. I would talk with a dainty ribaldry and offer to share the feast.

For shadow-things piled too near God compensates me in unexpected midnights with a Cold Boiled Potato: along with it a pantry doorway to stand in and a little glass salt-shaker to hold in my other hand.

*

The Strange Braveness

If God has human feelings he must often have a burning at the eyes and a fullness at the throat at the strange Braveness of human people: their Braveness as they go on in the daily life, with aching dumbish minds and disgruntled bereft bodies and flattened pinched gnawed hearts.

The easy human slattern way would be to sink beneath the burden.

Instead, people: I and Another and all others - seamstresses and monotonous clerks and lawyers and housewives: sit upright in chairs and talk into telephones and walk fast and eat breakfasts and brush hair: all the while marooned in a morass of small wild unexciting tasteless Pain.

Of others - what do I know?

But I might say, "Look, God, I am not fallen on the ground, from this and that - utterly lost and down. But sitting, drooping but strong, in a chair, mending a lamp-shade - neat, orderly, and at-it in my misery."

*

Just Beneath My Skin

This I write is a strange thing.

So close to fact: so far from it.

So close to truth: so surrounded by lies.

It does not contain lies but is someway surrounded by a mist of lies.

A strange thing about it is that it is expressing the Self Just Beneath My Skin.

That Self is someways trivial and outlandish and mentally nervous, flightly, silly - silly to a verge of tragicness. I know that to be true from a long acquaintance with me. It is oddly intriguing to read over some chapters and find it *shown*.

Some unconscious exact photography aids my writing talent.

Some chapters are bewilderingly and mysteriously true to life.

My everyday self that casually speaks to this or that person is nothing like this book. My absorbed self that writes a letter to an intimate acquaintance is not like this book. My heartfelt self that deeply loves a friend, and gives of its depths, and thrills answeringly to other depths, is not like this book.

This book is my mere Hidden Self - just under the skin but hid away closer than the Thousand Mysteries: never shown to any other person in any conversation or any association: never would be shown: never could be.

How Another, any Other, would come out: what Another would show: photographed Beneath the Skin - what do I know?

Perchance ten times more trivial and inconsequent and mad than Me.

If Another thinks Me someway mad, let him look at Himself Just Beneath the Skin.

Perchance Another every day as he thanks a janitor for holding open a door, would much prefer to drive a long rusty brad-nail deep into the janitor's skull.

Perchance Another has a brain like Goethe, a Soul like a humming-bird, a Heart like a little round nutmeg.

What do I know?

I know what I am.

Another may know what he is.

But I can't tell Me to Another and Another can't tell Himself to Me.

I can tell Me to myself and write it.

Another if he reads will see Me: but not as I see Me. Instead, through many veil-curtains and glasses, very darkly.

*

God's Kindly Caprice

To-morrow

For twenty-five cents and one hour and twelve minutes one may get in this present detailed world a bit of unforgettable complete enchantment.

So I found to-day in a moving-picture theater. A Carmen, the real Carmen of Prosper Mérimée glowed, vibrated, lived, and died with passion on a white screen.

Of all prose writers I know Prosper Mérimée is the one - (intimate and sensitively alive as if I had lain against his shoulder as I read *La Guzla* and "Venus d'Ille" - he melts into my veins -) whom I would most eagerly see interpreted. Of all fiction characters - if she is fiction - the poignant Carmen is the one I would most eagerly see realized.

Carmen is one of those fictions which are truer to life than life is. Such fiction-things are all around, touching everybody: the spoken truths which grow false at being spoken: the thought lies which turn to truths the moment they touch words.

I have heard Carmen sung and seen her filmed by the lustrous Farrar, and I have seen her play-acted by some lesser lights. But Bizet's opera, a sparkling music-storm, creates a sonant objective Carmen, a beautiful bloody lyric, remote from Mérimée who made a Carmen intensely peculiar to his own subjective art. And the stage-Carmen has always been a stage-Carmen waiting in dusty draughty wings for her cues. It remained for the cinematograph, which is a true literal mirror of human expression, to make Carmen burst into violent physical life.

But it was less the scopes of the films which made Carmen animate than it was the virile woman who played her. It was acting - but acting in the sense of losing and sinking and saturating and dissolving herself in another woman's temperament: and by it she achieved some strong sword-keen shadings of the Carmen character - to the hair's-breadth.

And she *looked* like Carmen. It was not important to the vigorous fire of her acting but it made bewitchment in the portrait. No one I have before seen play Carmen fitted the elusive points of her description.

"Her eyes were set obliquely in her head but they were magnificent and large. Her lips, a little full but beautifully shaped, revealed a set of teeth as white as newly-skinned almonds. Her hair was black with blue lights on it like a raven's wing, long and glossy. To every blemish she united some advantage which was perhaps all the more evident by contrast. There was something strange and wild about her beauty. Her face surprised you at first sight but nobody could forget it. Her eyes especially had an expression of mingled sensuality and fierceness which I had never seen in any human glance. Gypsy's eye, wolf's eye -"

This (from the English translation of the story by Lady Mary Loyd) fitted to a charm the pictured vision of the foreign-looking woman - her name is Theda Bara - who flung a throbbing Carmen across the screen with inde-scribable heat and color and luster. It was comparable only to the muscular force of the original which that Mérimée rubs nervously and heavily into one's thoughts. I felt it someway satisfyingly unbelievable - an illusion more actual than actuality: a dream which outbore fact.

I suppose there's no other character like Carmen for flaming roundness in all fiction: filled with her treacheries yet purely true to herself, without fear, utterly game: fierce, coarse, ruthless, and reckless yet wrapped in a maddening unwitting pathos: strong and bold and cruelly poised yet capable of sudden complete surrender: ignorant and abandoned and criminal in every instinct yet beyond every littleness, every pettiness: sensual yet contemptuous and indifferent in it, a woman of essential chastity. Carmen is the one criminal conception in whom there is no vulgar evil, no personal maculateness though wrecking all the wildness of her temper in her tempestuous days'-journeys. She is a romantic murderous appeal to human superjudgment. It was this isolate quality of her which Theda Bara gave out with mystic masterful art. She gauged the personal odors and blood-pressures of Carmen. She slipped into Carmen's skin and first sucked in and then breathed out the irresistible menacingness and arresting ruination of her beautiful diabolic spirit. A little feverish artistic thrill ran in my veins as I sat in the dark watching.

"She had thrown her mantilla back," says Don José in the translated tale, "to show her shoulders and a great bunch of acacias that was thrust into her chemise. She had another acacia bloom in the corner of her mouth and she walked along swaying her hips like a filly from the Cordova stud farm. In my country anyone who had seen a woman dressed in that fashion would have crossed himself. In Seville every man paid her some bold compliment on her appearance. She had an answer to each and all with her hand on her hip -. 'Come, my love,' she began again, 'make me seven ells of lace for my mantilla, my pet pin-maker.' And taking the acacia blossom out of her mouth she flipped it at me with her thumb so that it hit me just between the eyes. I tell you, sir, I felt as if a bullet had struck me."

This first meeting of Carmen with the dragoon was pictured in a brilliant hot-looking plaza as if before the cigarette factory in Seville. This woman in throwing the flower at the soldier expressed wonderfully in one fleet moment, by hand and lip and eye, the savage sordid poetry and passionate freedom - that unearthly fragrance - which *is* Carmen.

The film version followed the scenes of the opera rather than the story, which took nothing from the headlong truth of the central figure.

But no picturing can equal the star-clarity of Mérimée's prose in Carmen's death-scene - a thing of a piercing pathos comparable to nothing I know in writing.

After we had gone a little distance I said to her, "So, my Carmen, you are quite ready to follow me, isn't it so?"

She answered, "Yes, I'll follow you to the death - but I won't live with you any more."

We had reached a lonely gorge. I stopped my horse.

"Is this the place?" she said.

And with a spring she reached the ground. She took off her mantilla and threw it at her feet, and stood motionless with one hand on her hip, looking at me steadily.

"You mean to kill me, I see that well," she said. "It is fate. But you'll never make me give in."

I said to her: "Be rational, I implore you, listen to me. All the past is forgotten. Yet you know it is you who have been my ruin - it is because of you that I am a robber and a murderer. Carmen, my Carmen, let me save you, and save myself with you."

"José," she answered, "what you ask is impossible. I don't love you any more. You love me still and that is why you want to kill me. If I liked I might tell you some other lie, but I don't choose to give myself the trouble. Everything is over between us two. You are my rom and you have the right to kill your romi, but Carmen will always be free. A calli she was born and a calli she'll die."

"Then you love Lucas?" I asked.

"Yes, I have loved him - as I loved you - for an instant - less than I loved you, perhaps. And now I don't love anything. And I hate myself for ever having loved you."

I cast myself at her feet. I seized her hands. I watered them with tears, I reminded her of all the happy moments we had spent together, I offered to continue my brigand's life, if that would please her. Everything, sir, everything - I offered her everything if she would only love me again.

She said: "Love you again? That's not possible. Live with you? I will not do it."

I was wild with fury. I drew my knife. I would have had her look frightened and sue for mercy - but that woman was a demon.

I cried: "For the last time I ask you, Will you stay with me?"

"No! No! No!" she said and she stamped her foot. Then she pulled a ring I had given her off her finger and cast it into the brushwood. I struck her twice over - I had taken Garcia's knife because I had broken my own. At the second thrust she fell without a sound. It seems to me that I can still see her great black eyes staring at me. Then they grew dim and the lids closed. - For a good hour I lay there prostrate beside the corpse. -

No play-acting could make the scene so pregnant and palpitant with human-stuff and alive in vision as that translucent jewel-prose of Mérimée. But so close as one art may counterfeit another, by drinking-up the fiery spirit essence which informs it, so close did this actor-woman compass and consummate the strong delicious unafraidness of Carmen's death-hour.

The scene was staged as in the opera - a court outside the bull-fighting arena, with Carmen richly bejeweled and dressed in the lacy smart-lady clothes of the Toreador's mistress. But that was nothing. The gypsy wildness of the written scene was in every insolently splendid bodily movement and each fateful loveliness of eyes and lips of the fulfilling Theda Bara.

I can still see the dark drooping-lidded dying eyes.

I sensed Carmen in conscious chambers of my Mind.

I felt her in my throat. It was Carmen herself living and breathing near me, the fearsomely adorable Carmen who has haunted the edge of my thoughts since I first read her.

There are some odd crudenesses in Theda Bara's acting which had the effect of making her un-stagey, unobvious. They made her humanly vibrant. And they added a devilish wistfulness to her Carmen and a surprising feel of genuineness to the whole masque.

The actor's art brings out the romance which is in human bone-and-flesh. And Theda Bara seems someway a master of its physical and spiritual subtleties. She expressed the swift emotion of Carmen by ringing slightest possible changes on her own virile and mobile body: insolence by kimboing an elbow: cruelty by the twitch of a wrist: sensual feeling by moving a knee and an ankle: murder in the twisting of her waistline: a fleet repressed animal tenderness by a posture of shoulder and breast: a heartbreak of mirth in her careless vivid lips: the desperate bravery of that death by the tilt of her potent chin: the hurricane-freedom of Carmen's soul by lifting her face and her arms in the night wind. She worked with an exquisite muscular sincerity, as if she strongly gave her best of brain and blood and mettle to the part.

I looked at photographs of her which decorated the lobby of the theater. She looks a beautiful and earnest-seeming girl of a mental rather than a physical caste, with melancholy dark eyes, a child-like mouth-profile and the slim patrician hands of a Bourbon duchess. She will live in my warmed memory as the star of all the Carmens.

A flood of life and color goes into the staging of a Carmen film: a throng of attractive faces and bodies of people, women and men and lovely children, move through it in a pulsating gay pageant: flowers and Spanish prettinesses of costume and country-side and street and café are all over it, bright as life: and sweet winds blow in it and leaves and grasses wave and flutter, and the sunshine melts and mellows the air - all as if one saw it thrice-enlarged through windows. It is not poetry - it is not in itself any art, but a dear delectable counterfeit of it, a miracle-*taste* of the outer-looking madly-peopled world.

For me it meant my long-adored Mérimée given sudden brief life, the haunting Carmen turned into flesh: a spell of silent human-music which glowed and burned upon me like gentle fire.

Often is God thus capriciously kind to me.

*

A Fascinating Creature

To-morrow

I am a fascinating creature.

I move in no stultifying ruts. There's no real yoke of custom on my shoulders. My round white breasts beneath their black serge are concurrent with nothing settled or subservient or discreet.

My Mind goes in no grooves made by other minds. It lives like a witch in a forest, weaving its spells, revelling in smooth vivid adventure. When I look at a round gray stone by a roadside I look at it not as a young woman, not as a person, not as an artist, nor a geologist, nor an economist, but as Me - as Mary MacLane - and as if there had not before been a round gray stone by a roadside since the world began. When I look at a chair with my somber eyes I say to the chair, "What other persons may see when they look at you, chair, I don't know - how could I know? But I well know what I see and that what I see is uninfluenced by other eyes that may have looked at you, were they Aristotle's or Galileo's or an archangel's." There may be equally egotistic viewpoints - in Waco-Texas, or Japan, or Glasgow-Scotland, or the Orkney Islands, where not? I don't know - I don't care. What is it to me? I know my own virile vision and that it thrills and informs and translates me as if crackling bright-jagged lightnings broke along my sky. -

It is a night of whispering breezes and little restless clouds, an endearing night. It makes solitude a delectation. I walked out in it, in the glimmering moonlight past buildings and houses and mines and mounds. My thoughts as I walked were all of Me: how fascinating is Me.

I came in at midnight and met Me in my mirror. I pushed my three-cornered hat backward off my head, slipped out of my loose coat, and dropped my squeezed gloves. I sank fatiguedly into a little chair before the mirror, tipped the chair forward on its front legs, rested my elbows on the bureau and my chin in my hands, and looked absorbedly at myself. Lovingly, tenderly, discerningly, marveling and absorbed and deeply fascinated I looked at Me in the mirror. "You enchanted one!" said I, "You Witch-o'-the-world! you Mary MacLane! - who you are *I* don't know - what you are I but partly know. You're my Companion, my Familiar, my Lover, my wilding Sweetheart - I love you! I know that - that's enough. I love your garbled temper, your aching thoughts, your troubled Heart, your wasted spirit. I know much, much, much of you and love you! I love your beauty-sense and your proud scornful secret super-sensitiveness. I love your Eyes and your Lips and your bodily Fire and Ice" -

- *to* know *oneself: apart from all the world!*

One looking at me sees a cold-poised young woman, reserved and aloof, slightly diffusing insolence and inspiring misgivings.

But I looking at Me see a woman standing high on flame-washed battle-ments of her life in whom burn and beat the spirits and lights and star-discords of uncounted tired lustrous ages. I see me forlorn and radiant, drab and brilliant. I see me wrapped in a fiery potentiality of pain and beauty and love and sorrow. I hear wild voices in Me like horrid-sweet wailing of ghost-violins, muted but crying loudly in frightful reasonless vital joy and in unspeakable terror and sadness. I see Me ragged-clothed, bleeding, with disordered tangled hair and bloodshot eyes, with coarse soiled hands, broken-nailed, like a criminal's: a woman of woes. And I see Me wistful in quiet pure garments like one seeking light. I see Me old as old sin and young as new Spring days. I see Me un-sanely sensitive and hardened over -closed in worldly cases: guarded antagonism round my thoughts, protecting indifference round my Heart, dead silence round my Soul. I see Me with brains to know, with prescient mind to grasp, with mobile sense to feel. I see Me all futile, all hopeless, all miserable. I see Me all poetry. I see Me all wonder, mystery, and beauty. I see Me! -

- *much more than that,* this *Me sitting here! my deep gray wanton dark eyes: my lips - like pink flowers - with the inscrutable expression: my white fingers - slim, strong, glossy-nailed, silken at the tips. My glass gives Me back to Me, sitting by it, languid of Body, tense of spirit and Mind, bathed in witcheries of Self -*

I love my Mary MacLane! Ah - I love her!
It is good - since I can't find God, since I can't find way-of-truth however I grope about.
Every human friendship I form throws me back more completely on myself.
Whom then shall I love but myself?
I know my own human enchantments and that they never fail me.
I'll know them more! I'll love them more! - I'll love them in sane madness lest mad madness overtake and destroy Me, Soul and bones.

*

No Resonance

To-morrow

My life, myself, I know are nothing noble, nothing constructive.
There is no resonance in this analysis, but all Dissonance.
Something lives, lives muscularly in me that constantly betrays me, de-stroys me against all my own convictions, against all my own knowledge,

against all my own desire.

It may be true of Everybody.

I don't know. I think about it but get nowhere.

It seems someway unlike God to make each person a something all of cross-purpose.

But I doubt that I am different from Everybody.

I doubt if I am anyway abnormal.

I am very sane.

A match-flame burns me the same as it burns Everybody: pins prick me and hurt.

Yet I look in myself and see, through harmonic details, the massed Dissonance.

I am dying in a pit.

*

Black-Browed Wednesdays

To-morrow

All my life I've liked the Back of a magazine.

Some black-browed Wednesday I purchase a magazine, a fifteen-cent one, and read it through. I read the stories and they deeply engage or lightly interest me. I read the "special articles" and if they tell about flying machines or wild birds or hospitals or woman-prisoners in penitentiaries they charm or absorb my thoughts. I look at the illustrations and try to decide whether they are art or science or mechanism. I read the verse and if it's poetry it exhilarates me as if closed shutters were opened to let Day into a gloomy Room.

Then I read the advertisements in the Back and they do all of those things to me in comforting life-giving oxygen-furnishing ways. Each advertisement is a short story with an eerie little "plot" in it: each is a special article full of purpose: each is fruitful poetry: and in my two hands I all-but have and hold those wonderful Things they exploit.

They make me feel it's my birthday and I'm presented a wealth of lavish gifts.

They make me feel it's all a world of playthings.

They make me feel like a baby with a rattle, a ball, and a hoop of bells.

I like *everything* in the Back of a magazine.

I like the Revolvers, handsome plausible short-barreled Revolvers with pictures of ordinary people in dim-lit midnight bedrooms, and ordinary expected-looking burglars climbing in windows - Revolvers of ten shots and of six, and of different calibers, and all of them gleamingly mystically desirable: I like the Soaps, smooth amorous appetizing Soaps, some in luxurious Paris packets, and others spread out in blue water and rosy foam, splashed in by athletic Archimedesque young men and fat creamy babies and slim beautiful ladies - Mary Garden Soap of pungent delicious scent, tar Soap for the long lovely hair of girls, austere Ivory Soap - it floats: I like the Rubber Heels of resilient charm so tellingly pictured and described that at once I desire them beneath my spirit-heels - springy and solid and thick and firm: I like the Tooth-pastes and Tooth-powders and Tooth-lotions in tubes and tins and bottles, each bearing beneficent messages to the human white teeth of this world - one unfailing kind coming lyrically out like a ribbon and lying flat on the brush: I like the foods - of miraculous spotless purity and enticement - Biscuits and Chocolate and Figs, and *Foie-gras* in thick glossy little pots, so richly pictured and sung that merely to let my thoughts graze in their pasturage fattens my Heart: I like the men's very thin Watches, and men's Garters - no metal can touch you -, and men's fluffy-lathered shaving sticks, and men's trim smart flawless tailored Suits, in none of which I have use or interest until I find them in the Back of a magazine - where at once they grow charming and romantic: I like the jars and boxes and tubes and glasses of Cold Cream, Cold Cream fit for skins of goddesses, fit for elves to feed on - a soft satiny scented snow-white elysium of wax and vaseline and almond paste, pictured in forty alluring shapes till it feels pleasantly ecstatic just to be living in the same world with bewitching vases of Cold Cream, Cold Cream, Cold Cream - always bewitching and lovely but never so notably and festively as in the Back of a magazine: and I like the Pencils: and Book-cases: and Silver: and Jewels: and Glass: and Gloves: and Shoes - beautiful Shoes: and Fountain-pens: and Leather things: and Paint - silkish salubrious Paints, house-Paints, and the panegyrics with them - they make me long to own a spirit-house and paint it liberally: and Rugs: and Varnish: and Clothes - wonderful Clothes: and Bungalows: and Phonographs - his master's voice: and Paper - fine-wrought Paper to write on - bond and linen and hand-pressed, pale-tinted - a vast virgin treasure: and Oranges: and Cigarettes - a shilling in London, a quarter here: and Water Bottles of powdery rubber: and Stockings - patrician Stockings which take me into realms of silk-looms and delicate dyes and slim ankles: and Candle-Shades: and Candle-Sticks: and countless Cosmetics - Cosmetics of tender colors for the outer woman: and Sealing-wax indescribably useless and attractive: and Tennis-Racquets: and Ivory - smooth Vantine Ivory toys and trinkets polished softly bright as moonlight - and their lily-worded descriptions like restrained sonnets: and Washing Powders - let the Gold Dust twins do your work: and Shower-baths: and Evans' Ale: and Flying Boats: and Umbrellas: and Cameras - if it isn't an Eastman it isn't a kodak: and boxes of Candy - sweet wilderness of chocolates - their very makers' names have a melting gust - Allegretti, Huyler, Clarence Crane, Maillard - cloying courtiers all: and Diamond Dyes - a child can use them: and Veranda Screens - she can look out but he can't look in: and Cedar Chests: and Chartreuse from Carthusian monasteries: and Perfumes - Perfumes in their maddening-sweet pride, Perfumes from Paris, Perfumes bottled in thick crystal, enchantingly costly - each American dollar added to their price-by-the-ounce making them fragranter to my thoughts: and boxes of benevolent Matches, and captivating Brooms, and fascinating Scouring-powders - a Dutch girl on the can chasing dirt - all three luscious tempting things in the Back of a magazine: and Automobiles - ask the man who owns one: and Rifles - simple and formidable and fine: and restful Rat-poison - they die in the open air seeking water: and sacks of Flour - eventually, why not now - flour unusual and piquant in the Back of a magazine, flour novel and endearing: and Type-writers: and Mushrooms: and Monkey-Wrenches: and Rosaries: and Rock-salt -

- the Back, the Back, the Back of a magazine -

There's no sadness and no terror in the Back of a magazine.

And it is for Everybody, Everybody.

A million people read a story in the middle of the magazine and half the million readily miss its point. But a single tin of Talcum Powder in the Back - the whole million note that and miss nothing in it: it gets to them both on and under their skin.

Some of the million read a ten-line poem in *vers libre* in the front of the magazine - and nine-tenths of their number are hard-put to it: the mentalities of this human race being mostly shops shut down. It is something pregnant and prophetic to a poet, merely musical to a plain prose writer, arrant folly to a telephone girl, amusing nonsense to a butcher, a comic fantasy to a milliner, a form of insanity to a plumber, an unknown tongue to a milk-man, a kind of sin to a Baptist minister. But to each of those a Can of Soup in the Back of the same magazine has easily, exactly the same ox-tail-ish meaning: it reaches them where they live.

A thousand persons agree with an article about atavism in orang-outangs and ten thousand more quite refute it. But they all harmoniously commit suicide with the same make of Revolver - hammer the hammer - or get rousing drunk to the same degree with the same brand of high-powered whiskey - Wilson, that's all.

A countess, a courtesan, and a convict-woman summarily pass over the front and middle of the magazine as containing nothing to their purpose. But like jungle denizens at their drinking pool the three of them meet hostilely on the common ground of a popular Cigarette featured in the Back - a blend to suit every taste - wherewith they unwittingly smoke away half their generic differentiations.

The Colonel's Lady and Judy O'Grady anoint themselves nightly into a state of shining invisible kinship from separated twin jars of the same bewitching Cold Cream.

I'm not sure myself and Miss Lily Walker of the Broadway chorus regard similarly a beauteous box of Rice Powder: she perchance would at once dash madly into it and powder herself o'er with it, whereas I would fain ponder about it awhile as a tiny be-violeted adventure. But pondering or powdering, equally exciting to each of us is its delicate pale lilac blazonment in the Back of a magazine.

The front of the magazine may mean little to you and the middle of the magazine may mean nothing to me: the Back of it none of us escapes.

It is for Everybody, Everybody.

Even Senegambians: they can look at the pictures and marvel over them.

I can there meet a Senegambian on the common ground of it might be a delicate transparent oval of Pears' Soap, pretty as a jewel of price: perchance we would each unconsciously feel we wouldn't be happy till we got it.

It's only as playthings I want the Things in the Back of a magazine.

To me they are toys, lyrics of matter, food of the senses.

The octroi would have no sympathy with my loiterings among their wares. It is a fete of my own, indolent and fanciful, unrecognized in commerce.

Any article I may put to its forthright use in actuality becomes an idyllic toy when I find it in the Back of a magazine. The desirable Revolvers are not firearms with which to shoot myself and burglars, but only bijous to have and handle and caress. The luxuriant vervain- and violet-scented Soaps are not for my toilet, but something to eat, for my astral body to feed on - nourishing food they make. The lush Cold Creams have no massaging possibilities in them - they are for my thoughts to gambol among, for my meddlesome spirit-fingers to touch and fuss with deliciously, blissfully, transcending all vulgar use. The men's thin Watches mean nothing to me as Watches: and their Garters - what's it to me whether no-metal-can-touch-you or no-metal-at-all? My thoughts merely revel and juggle with them, picture and legend - they are pastimes of my child-self. The cream-woven Note Papers are not to write on but wherewithal to imagine how cool and smooth they would feel drawn slowly across my flushed cheek. A sack of Flour - I feel only how I'd like to have it spilled out - eventually-why-not-now - in a thick warm-tinted heap on the blue-velvety floor of my room that I might roll and bathe in it and feel it feathery-fluffy on my skin.

So I play with my toys on black-browed Wednesdays.

Some Wednesdays even fail to be black-browed because there are Backs to magazines.

*

The Conscious Analyst

To-morrow

I don't know whether I write this because I wear two plain dresses or whether I wear two plain dresses because I write it.

My life fell into a lowering mood which calls for but two dresses: which mood compels me to write out these things that are in me as inevitably as heavy gathered clouds come raining to the ground. The mood having overtaken me I can not keep from writing this day after day, more than I can keep from brushing my hair every day, and eating lumps of food every day, and picking up tiny white specks from my blue rug.

I love this book and I fear and hate it. I love the writing of it though it is a finical unobvious task - more so than it looks. And often I fear to read it over lest I hurt my own feelings. And I hate it in ways. I am a particularly sane woman when all's said. And many things I come to in me are grating and inexplicable and incongruous. But also I love it. It is my companion "when the world is gone." I am as solitary as if I had no human place in this earth. My days are as silent as if I lived in it alone. The few voices that bespeak me in a day or a week stop at my ear-drums and are immensely alien. At times, for weeks on end, I am quite alone in this house and the silence then has a depth and a hollowness. From it I feel not alone in a house but alone in a world: and more when the family is in the house.

And it is what-should-I-do if I had not a writing talent to expend me upon from day to day, and so rest me. I feel God around some corner but that feeling is no rest, but only an odd terror which wants the dignity of terror.

Times I wonder if I shall have this published afterward for all to read and if so what colors it will paint on my world - and what else may befall.

But it's an aspect dim and remote now. I wearing but two nunlike dresses and face to face with me, have nothing to do with publishing books and with the beautiful noisy world and its befallings. It is easy to believe I shall never again have to do with any of that. This may be my death-mood. I am very tired. The weight of being a person is heavy on me as weights of lead. And still I know if I suddenly bloomed with beautiful frocks and went out to-morrow to lose myself among people, people, people I should at once achieve a veneer of the utmost frivol. I have an odd frivolous quality full of an ardor and strength, with all of my mental mettle in it. Also I know if I did that now it would be but postponing this analytic reckoning. Which would confront me again with the more rancor, the more futileness gathered into it from having been put off.

This book and the two dresses are my present portion. If I could escape them (I am not quite sure I want to - but - *hell!*) - it would be of no use. They would come back again in an unexpected ripeness of time and demand a hearing: an exquisite nervous tragic hearing.

They are such stuff as the conscious analyst is made of.

But though I'm the conscious analyst I can't quite tell whether I write the book because I wear two plain black dresses or I wear those because I write it.

*

Eye When I Mean Tooth

To-morrow

I write it, and it's a surprising book.

It is not what on the surface it looks to be.

I do not write what my clear Mind may want to say to the white blank paper.

I do not write what my thoughts are saying to me.

Those things are facile, uninformed - flat mental pictures, the writer's craft.

I write what still voices of life - voices trivially frightful in their secret pettiness - voices of all my life - merest living - say to my ancient Soul and my young present Body and what they two may answer.

I am in some sort a wonderful person - and in places I do that, nearly perfectly.

I am also tired and someway whelmed by self-conscious despair, and possessed of a talent imperfect and inadequate to reveal the radiances and shades my being perceives: and in places I fail.

I fail remarkably. I write Eye when I mean Tooth. I write Fornicate when I mean Caress. I write Wine when I mean Blood. For no better reason than that my writing hand is not sufficiently dexterous: the little flashing shutters open and shut so quick that the second ones are shut and the third starting to open before I have got written the things I saw through the first ones. Only not always.

*

A Wild Mare

To-morrow

Also I am dissatisfying to myself.

My thoughts smother me: they keep me from life.

I am a hundred times more introspective than most people, most women. Most women, even conventional ones, are lawless - the more conventional, the more lawless usually.

And so most women beat me to life. Where they yield to an impulse the moment they feel it - I, because an impulse itself is adventure-fabric - I feel of its quality, test it for defects, wash a little corner of it to see if the color will run - and conclude not to use it.

That I gaze inward at the garbled biograph of Me keeps me from several sorts of violent action.

I have violent action in me, chained in analysis.

Most women are secretly lawless on the old plan inaugurated by Eve - of inclining to do anything forbidden, of hugging everything they are unsupposed to hug, of determinedly kicking over the traces when coerced too much. The ban is the chief attraction.

It's but little like that with me. There would be point and purpose in my Action. But it is kept in stupor by analysis.

I am malcontent about that, though I live upon analysis. I hate the inaction and inertia that follow on its heels.

I could be an anarchist. I condemn anarchists but not as I condemn Me. I would respect me more were I this moment prisoned in a real bastile for having stuck a good knife into a bad king. I could feel, no matter how foolish and mistaken in itself the act, that I had done the strong and brave thing at sacrifice of my personal selves. The dry living-death of the prison would be compensated for each day when I said to Me, "It was a needful honorable act and *I* did it: for once in my life I was a Regular Person."

There would be a nourishment in being able to tell that to myself. There would be warming food in owning one so brave remembrance of myself.

But, my Soul-and-bones! - at the very moment of lifting the good knife a thought would come: "How is this king worse than another? What rotten rascal mightn't rise in his place?" And on with a lightning-trail of analysis till my pale hand dropped inert and the knife in it grew harmless as a lily-petal.

It isn't that I haven't the guts. I have.

I am a wild mare in foal: and unfoaling.

*

The Mist

To-morrow

Because I am to myself someways dissatisfying and exasperating often this thing I write is dissatisfying and exasperating.

It is a true account of what is inside me. "The wine must taste of its own grapes."

It would be easier to make it an untrue account, for fiction is the most effortless of writing. So I have found it. And I am very clever.

I could write myself as a pretty dainty harmlessly purring one - the leopard with claws clipped and fangs drawn.

When my dynamos rest I am like that, doubtless.

But the wears and tears of breathing and the influences of varied life-details and of clothes worn and food eaten start me moving devilishly.

Phases of a score of persons, men and women, come to light in me.

To be one human being means to be monstrously mixed.

I write me out not as I might be, nor as I should be - whatever that may be -: but merely as I am.

As, Just Beneath The Skin, I am.

So my written account must come out someways dissatisfying and ex-asperating. Logically dissatisfying and divinely and ethically exasperating.

- a passage in Virgil tells of a Mist that is all over and about this world from the human "tears that are falling, falling, falling always." Something, and it may be that Mist, makes one's view of everything - everything in life - a little blurred. It may even blur one's view of oneself. So it may be I do not see myself with entire clearness -

I only know I write me as clearly as I see me, considering the Mist.

*

A White Liner

To-day came the Finn woman and cleaned my blue-and-white bedroom.

She comes now and again and cleans excellently.

I would like to clean my room myself but lack the strength and skill to do it well.

But I stay with the Finn woman and show her how and I watch her work and muse upon her. She would be called in England a charwoman, but in this America of the vast mongrel heterogenesis she is an unclassified laborer.

I like to watch her and talk with her a bit and dwell on her mixed potentialities. She contrasts fascinatingly with me.

She is a human being and so am I, and beyond and with that there are odd parallels and similarities and distinctions between her and me.

Her name is Josephina and she looks as if it might be.

Mine is Mary MacLane but I don't look entirely like it.

She lives a lonely life and so do I, differing in sort and circumstance.

I am middle-class and American of Canadian reminiscence, and early-thirty.

Josephina is Finn and lower-class with a "foreign" look, and she is forty-five and looks sixty and is twelve years out of Finland.

I am tallish and slim and weigh nine wavering stone.

The Finn woman is short and solid and weighs all of a hundred and seventy pounds.

I am slender of flank and ankle, narrow through the loins and bony at the shoulders.

The Finn woman is thick everywhere, broad of girth and deep of chest like a Percheron stallion.

I am darkish with dusky gray eyes.

Josephina is dirty-blond with pale narrow blue eyes like a china doll's.

My sex feels to me like a mysterious sweetness.

Josephina's sex looks porcinely obvious and uninteresting like her large dubious breasts.

I am inwardly full of strong-flavored emotions.

The one positive outward feeling Josephina manifests is a dull but comprehensive hatred, peculiar to her nationality and station, for everything Swedish.

The Finn woman has a husband now and had a different one formerly.

I have none and never had.

Josephina is elemental primeval woman.

So am I but terrifically qualified by complexity, incongruity.

I have white smooth firm beautiful hands.

Josephina's hands are particularly ugly and have a menacing look.

I have quick intelligence.

Josephina is markedly stupid.

I live in a quiet clean bungalow.

Josephina lives in an unusually filthy unrestful little house.

I own two dresses whose personnel alters at intervals.

Josephina owns one unchanging dress, septic, maculate, and repellent.

I have a sense of humor vivid and intriguing to myself.

Josephina has no more sense of humor than a flat-iron.

I bathe foamily icily each morning.

Josephina would seem never to have had a bath.

She cleans windows and floors and rugs for thirty-five cents an hour. She would regard it as a fantastic waste of time and soap to clean herself for nothing.

I own in a still flawed life one phase which is an endless treasure of beauty and power and charm and light: my love for John Keats.

The Finn woman owns about the same thing in a life which may be more still and flawed than mine: her love for strong drink.

There begins a curious line of similitude between us.

I feel oddly joyous and light of heart on a solitary veranda corner with the John-Keats poetry book open in my lap.

And Josephina has been found many a time by Butte policemen sitting alone joyous and very drunk, in dark alleys with empty pint bottles strewn all about her.

In my un-Keats hours I am mostly mournful. And Josephina sober has all the melancholy of her race with an added gloom, as if the acetylene had run out of all her lamps. That my melancholy is more lustrous than hers I lay to her native dullness as against my native braininess, and to alcohol's having rotting effects on human mental tissues: whilst John Keats to those who drink his poetry is a starry savior.

I like to think there's the same ambrosial food in the Demon Rum for Josephina as in the Grecian Urn for me.

There seems no other pleasure in life for her.

The limit of her literary pursuit is the reading of a four-page Finnish newspaper full of obituaries.

The opalescent enchantments of her inner being mean nothing to her: she wouldn't know her entity from her duodenum.

Her body can bring her no delight: there's no lightness to it, no tang, no feminine charm, no consciousness to make her love it as the Dianas love theirs.

A sunset above the western peaks is less than a setting sun to her.

Her food is merely her fodder.

Love and Romance pass her by. She and the husband vie with each other for solitary possession of their little nasty house. And her personality is not conducive to lovers.

She has nor chick nor child to mother.

Her idea of a life beyond this vale is crude and uncomfortable. She went two Sundays to the Finnish church and had a surprising lusty doctrine of eternal fire rammed down her throat: she took the Finn minister's word for it and quitted the fold, preferring to live this life unhampered by flaming anticipation.

All her material treasure she works for with mops and scrubbing-brushes at thirty-five cents an hour.

Other roads being thus blocked it is sing-ho for King Alcohol in pint bottles.

Josephina is what is called a white liner. Which means that she has drunk so long, so much, so regularly that whiskey, rum, gin, and brandy have no or negligible effects upon her. To achieve her intoxicating aim she must drink pure alcohol.

By the same token I eschew many a tame poet: I must have John Keats.

What the poetry of John Keats does to me I know.

What the distilled waters of her choice do to Josephina it pleases me to imagine while I watch her clean my walls and floor and windows.

She works strongly, steadily, quietly till I pronounce the room clean. Then she stops, carries the pails and other things downstairs to the kitchen, removes a big brass pin from the rear of her dingy skirt which had held it back and doubled over her darkling petticoat, re-dons an antique rain-coat and bad hat, ties her clinking silver into the corner of a decadent handkerchief, bids me good-evening with a grave blond Finn bow and goes out into the dusk. She takes her way through alleys and short-cuts to the side door of a "Finlander" gin-palace in the Finn quarter of the town. And there she lays out her day's wage in the pint bottles of her delight. As many pint bottles as her few dollars will buy, so many she buys. She ventures her all in the name of passionate thirst taking no thought of the morrow. She then seeks out some alley with a dark door-step and there she does her drinking. It would not do to go home with her alcoholic wealth because the husband might be there who, like the alphabetic vintner, would "drink all himself." So she drinks away in pint-bottle-ish peace, sitting alone in the gloom of the alleyway door-step, in her limp rain-coat and bad hat and her stolid

Finn self-sufficience.

Because I like Josephina it charms me to think of the happiness that must be hers as she sits emptying pint bottles into herself and the white strong firewater begins to work.

Before having her drinks she is unelated and uninformed like a corpse coldly electrified by a storage battery. As she drinks and drinks on she remains outwardly unchanged as the way is with her race - but within! The changes that come to pass in the heavy person of Josephina as the white flames wash down her walls!

Into her dull veins pours a hot stream like melted seething copper and it heats her knees till she knows she *has* knees and that they are white and very beautiful: and it heats her legs and her back and her breasts till they glow with the double-glow of an Aphrodite's in a reluctant Adonis' arms: it heats her eyes and temples and throat till she feels herself a radiant girl: it heats the crown of her head till she feels something like a brain there: it heats her heart and stomach till she's filled with a gay gust for life: it heats her imagination till she even imagines herself in love with her hard Finn husband since he is not by to beat her and so dispel the fancy: it heats a sense of humor into her till she laughs suddenly and heartily at some fugitive funniness that had lain long frozen in her memory: it heats a hundred little human carburetors in her which send a wreathe of vapors up into her drab being to flush it with misty golds and thin blues and rosy crimsons till her dormant involuntary soul awakes - a thing of old mellowed beauty, it may be - and is wafted on warm pretty vapory wings far from alleys, far from mops and scrubbing brushes, far from thirty-five cents an hour, far from doorsteps - to fair sweet Isles of the Blest!

Nearing the last of her pint bottles she reels sideways on the door-step: her bad hat cants forward: she sprawls about. The policeman on that beat to whom in that aspect she is a figure long familiar strolls toward her late in the night and looks at her with a lackluster eye. But Josephina is physically unaware of all this world. Her last pint bottle is gamely emptied, her inner sun's chromosphere burns like mad - but her body, unable to cope with the virile delectations new-risen within it, limply gives way.

A quaint picture, interesting to dwell on: her thick bathless body laid low in the darkened alley, with the empty pint bottles scattered on the paving-stones beside it - but her astral shape, lit by the subtle fires of alcohol, lifted high, high to remote elysiums. The policeman calls the "wagon" and Josephina is taken up by several ungentle hands and tossed into it like a sack of coal. They take her to the city jail and lock her in a cell. The next morning she stands jaded and morbidly intoxicated before a police judge who glances at her uninterestedly for the several-hundredth time and says five days.

The five days can not be pleasant days but Josephina owns a robust sporting spirit. She gives not so much as the shrug of a shoulder either at going into jail or coming out of it. A black eye from her husband, a broken arm from a drunken fall, a filthy sojourn in jail: all one to her. She accepts them as she accepts all of her life, with an immense psychic calm. But she takes strongly to drink to translate herself out of it. And let her drink.

I know how she feels for I take to John Keats.

I don't myself care much for strong drink. I drink a little of it at irregular intervals, but, by and large, I drink without éclat. In this mountain altitude whiskey makes me sick, champagne makes me dizzy, and gin is a pungent punishment. One morning after reading of Josephina's white-line distinction in a police-court column I tasted some alcohol, but it had a varnish flavor and had strangling effects on my throat. It made me marvel at Josephina's prowess. I like absinthe in its bitter strength mostly because to sit sipping it feels restfully forbidden. Port wine is a brackish medicine, I hate the stickiness of cordials, and a cocktail I like chiefly to contemplate. So much for me and strong drink.

Josephina on the other hand does not care for John Keats. I sounded her on poetry in some of its human aspects: there was nobody at home. Her own enlightened north-country has some poets of borealic iron and brain-brawn and beauty: to Josephina's wooden intellect their books are eternally closed.

But the Demon Rum looses a heated flood of poetry upon her, which I can but vision and not feel.

I am incapable of strong drink even as Josephina is incapable of John Keats. We are quits there.

I look on myself as the more fortunate. - John Keats!

A woman so drunk as to fall and reel about is always an exquisitely shameful thing. And when I think of how she's tossed into the wagon - to mention but one item -

But it's a matter of the human equation. Doubtless it is all relative. The Finn woman is not aware of how she is knocked about, and if she were she would not regard it with any of my imagination. So what matter?

A likeable and admirable person is Josephina. A so strong fine business-like worker, a so thorough-bred sport, a so splendid drunkard, and asking no odds of God or man. In her stolid Finn fashion she likes me as she has proven, and I like her though she makes me feel inferior.

- if Josephina could and would write *her* inner isolated world of thoughts - the saga of her one horrid gown! There would be a book. All blacks and carmines - all stolidly sober and brilliantly drunk - all dingily bathless:

deeply savagely quietly human.

It would be a book savoring not of white alcohol but of the salty unshed Tears, the dry artistic Griefs of Josephina.

*

Beneficent Bedlam

To-morrow

I have been so long Sane it would be gay and sweet and resting to go Mad.

I would I could go Mad.

To a Mad-woman a Door is not a Door, probably: a Cat is not a Cat, belike: and To-morrow is not To-morrow at all - it may be week-before-last, it may be next year, it may be an exquisite jest. One can not tell *what* it is.

It is the thing one escapes by going Mad: Monotony.

It's all beneficent bedlam.

*

A Deadly Pathos

To-morrow

I love the sex-passion which is in this witching Body of me. I love to feel its portent grow and creep over me, like a climbing vine of tiny red roses, in the occasional dusks.

It is not shame or shadow or sordidness: but beauty and sweetness and light.

- *no token of sin: a token of virtue.*
- *no thing to crush: rather to nurture, to garner.*
- *no thing to forget: to remember, to think about.*
- *no flat weak drawn-out prose: live potent clipped heated poetry.*
- *not common and loosely human: rare and divine.*
- *not fat daily soup: stinging wine of life.*
- *not valueless because born of nothing and nowhere: valuable, priceless, a treasure under lock and key.*

Sex-desire comes wandering in dusk-time and gulfs me as in a swift violent sweet-smelling whirlwind.

It goes away sudden-variant as it came, out of a region of hot quick shadows.

And for that, for hours and days afterward, oranges and apples look brighter-colored to my eyes: hammocks swing easier as I sit in them: rugs feel softer to my feet: the black dresses lend themselves gentler to my form: pencils slide faciler on paper: my voice speaks less difficultly into telephones: meanings sound super-vibrant in Keats' Odes: sugar - little pinches of granulated sugar - are sharper, sweeter-sweeter in my throat.

And God grows less remote. And my wooden coffin and deep wet yellow clay grave move a long way back from me.

- all from fleeting ungratified wish of sly sex-tissues -

Also in it, and in my life from it, I sense some deathly pathos.

*

The Necklace

To-morrow

The necklace which God long ago hung round the white neck of my Soul is composed of little-seeming curses, like precious and semi-precious gems. They are polished smooth as if by age, as if by wear, as if by fingering, and as if by brisk industrious rubbing.

The Necklace is at once beautiful and ugly. The gems are in color chiefly blues and greens - with grays, lavenders, drabs, and mauves. But mostly blues and greens. They make a circlet of small stones strung at short intervals as if on a strong thin gold wire, with two large tawdry pretty pendants hung in front. One of the pendants is my fertile phase of Weakness and the other my odd encompassing Folly. The smaller stones are seventeen in number and their names and natures are these:

- the first is Dishonesty which makes ghosts of half my life.

- the second is Pretense, hard and genuine stone, which keeps me from being all-ways sincere even to anyone who knows me and whom I know: who loves me and whom I love.

- the third is Fear which makes me who scorn all leonine dangers cringe and crawl for trifles of life incredibly little.

- the fourth is Sensuality which burns and bursts across my Mind, half-missing my Body.

- the fifth is Anxiety, strange flawed green stone - by it I worry, tortured and wildly wavering, about the passing hours of my life: where they are going, where they are taking me.

- the sixth is Amativeness, extraordinary deep-tinted warm false gem -

it makes me love someway amorously some person I meet and fancy: an intimate tragedy, crucial and trivial.

- the seventh is Fatigue of the spirit itself, gray sad stone, meaning terrible sensations of age in my young flesh.

- the eighth is Incongruity, the sense and feeling of it, round blue stone - it kills what might be art and constructiveness and excellence in me.

- the ninth is Acquiescence, worn dull stone - it has kept me all the ages from the salvation of heated luminous strife.

- the tenth is Sensitiveness, pale-toned stone - by it the fingers of life touch me too suddenly, too sharply, too tensely to do me the good they might.

- the eleventh is Doubt, frail opalescent stone - by it my delight in the sunny Spring wind against my cheek is qualified with dubious surprise: by it I half-disbelieve in moon and stars and in long country roads stretched out solitary, lovely, drenched in sunset.

- the twelfth is Self-consciousness, blue-and-green stone - it robs me of the comfort and self-respect of feeling any motive in me to be un-ulterior.

- the thirteenth is Introspection, beautiful-beautiful blue-green stone - it pays for its place in beauty but by it I lose the building, the substance, the *matter* of living.

- the fourteenth is Intensity - too vivid vision, too vivid taste for some details of life - little hot-looking cool-feeling stone - by it I undervalue and overvalue, dwell upon surfaces, missing the serene feel and possession of precious solidness.

- the fifteenth is Isolation, pale purple stone - it makes me feel *never* at home, *never* at ease, *never* belonging - a subtle insulation - in this sheltered peopled world.

- the sixteenth is Bewilderment, mixed-tinted stone - by it I wonder *what* is truth with truth seeming that moment fluttering soft-plumed wings at my throat.

- the seventeenth is - it has no name - the *Feel-of-Me*, bright blue-green stone, lovely and loathesome - by it I've lost my way, I've felt all and only Me when I might have groped outward, hand and foot, and found a wind-swept path to go in: I was always blurred by Me.

A small Necklace, all dull gleams and unusual tints, strung finely and strongly and beautifully on shining gold. The sweet Soul droops like a wilted lily under even its slight weight. Strong fine rivets hold it firm-clasped and the weight of the two charming imitation pendant-stones keep it gracefully in place.

My loved and lovely Soul has worn it through the ages: manacle, shackle.

How long more - God may know but does not tell me.

It's only a Necklace. And my Soul is a Soul!

Even under the frail galling burden of the flesh the Soul of me to-morrow could tear off that Necklace and crumble it to airless nothing.

It does not: but *could*.

*

Slyly Garbling and Cross-Purposing

To-morrow

At rarish intervals comes my Soul to visit me.

My Soul is light sheer Being.

My Soul is like a young most beautiful girl marked and worn by long cycles of time but not anyway aged. She comes dressed in something like gray-white de-soie muslin or fine-grained crêpe silk, a loose-belted frock reaching to her ankles.

My Soul is unmoved by the world and the flesh and their feeling, as befits a Soul. She looks on me with a chill faëry-ish contempt, as also befits a Soul.

The quality of her contempt is of weary understanding and is like a caress.

In the dusk of yesterday came my Soul to visit me - a dusk of a deep beauty. The last glow of the sun lay along the earth, and all was gentian blue.

I leaned against my window-pane watching it, and beside me sat her Presence. Her Presence makes me feel wonderfully gifted: it is *mine*, this Soul all Golden-Silk and Silken-Gold!

We talk on many topics, of many things: I in worldly nervous ignorance and with a wishfulness to reach and compass and know: the Soul with poise and surety of attitude, a wearied patience and the chill sweet contempt.

She answers me from her cool old tranquil view-point, which is near me yet remote.

We talked last of some bygone persons I have been, some shapes she wore.

Said the Soul: "Early in the sixteenth century you were a ragged Russian peasant girl living in ignorance and filth in a hut by a swamp-edge. You had parents both of whom beat your body black-and-blue from your babyhood. And at eighteen you were a coarsened hardy wench tending a drove of pigs and goats on the sunny steppe. I was there with you as presently as now - as sentient, as perceptive. But it is a question whether you or the little beasts you drove were the more beastly stupid. You and they were equal in outer quality, equal in uncleanliness, equally covered with vermin."

I have no ghost-memory of that time, but as the Soul told of it a nascent feeling came on me, as if some part of my Mind felt its way back to that.

I warmed to the thought of the Peasant Girl. I was quiescent to her filth and ignorance.

Said I: "Was she brave and fairly honest?"

Said the Soul: "You were a ready liar - you lied your way out of many a beating. But you were brave enough. You faced the roughnesses of your life uncringing, and you died game."

Said I: "How did I die?"

Said the Soul: "You were run neatly through the body by the short sword of a soldier whose lust-desire you had had the hardihood to refuse - and I fled away upon the instant."

Said I: "I half-knew it - she died a violent death. You - were you glad to be quit of her filthy flesh, her surroundings, her ignorance?"

Said the Soul: "Glad? Such things mean nothing to me. Your body, be it sweet or foul, has no bearing on my long journey. Motives - motif - back of your human acts make me glad or sorry at leaving you."

Said I: "Tell me about a time when I seemed someway fine, humanly fine."

Said the Soul: "In London, near the end of the seventeenth century, before and during the period of the Gordon Riots, you lived in a way of peace. From when you were fourteen until you were twenty-nine you lived alone with your little lame half-sister whom you cared for very devotedly, very tenderly."

My little half-sister - Until the Soul spoke of her there was no vision, no image like her. Then something of me remembered.

Said I: "What was she like? Who were our parents?"

Said the Soul: "Your mother died at your birth, hers at her birth. Your father was hanged at Tyburn for forgery. The sister was pale, large-eyed, long-haired, crippled from a dislocated shoulder and hip. When you were twenty-five she was eleven, a beautiful frail child. You lived in two rooms above a linen-draper's and you supported the two of you by weaving and calendering cloths for the shop-keeper, and by illuminating missals and manuscripts when you could get that work. For a very poor wage, but living was cheap. All the time you took zealous care of your sister. Your heart was bound up in her - you adored her."

Said I: "I know that. Tell me what we did - how we lived - how we loved each other."

Said the Soul: "In the summer evenings you often walked out along quiet London streets - the sister sometimes with a crutch and your arm about her, sometimes in a rolling chair, whilst you walked beside her pushing it. Your father had educated you in an erratic fashion. You had a deal of desultory knowledge - what is called knowledge - and you educated the young sister in the same manner. Often it was of the poets - Latin, English, Italian - and of histories and sciences and arts - what odd comprehensive bits you knew - that you two talked as you sauntered in the bright late English sunlight. Or you talked of the little details of your joint life. Sometimes you sat together - you holding her close in your arms - by a window in your darkening front room, and watched the children at play in the common opposite, and conversed and were quietly happy. You were maternal and the child was a mature old-fashioned yet childish innocent child."

My little sister - sweet - long gone - Would that I had her now!

Said I: "Tell me what we said."

Said the Soul: "You said to her, 'Our poverty and even our deprivations, dearest, which for your sake I feel deeply would not matter, not the least, to me if I could see you well and strong.' And the child replied, 'Sweet, just to rest like this in your arms each twilight makes me rich, rich - as rich as the smartest ladies in Piccadilly.' And you said, 'Rich reminds me, Darling, we shall have four extra shillings - four bright silver shillings - at the end of this week from the book-seller. So what shall we purchase for a treat? There'll be, if you like, prawns and crumpets for tea, for days to come - or if my Child prefers oranges or pineapples once -' And the child replied with her cheeks quite pink at the thought, 'O Sister-love, let us have the pines, just one day, and let us make-believe to be ladies that day, and comport ourselves like ladies, and take our tea - all like ladies.' And you pressed her close to your breast - you both wore caps and kerchiefs and stuff-gowns in the fashion of the lower-middle artisan class - and showered gentle kisses on her cheeks and eyelids, and promised her the pineapples and the tea like ladies."

I listened to this with vivid still pleasure. It felt like endearing fulfilling life - a day of tenderness -. And oddly familiar.

Said I: "What were we in the habit of having for our tea - that prawns and crumpets would make us a treat?"

Said the Soul: "Your tea was chiefly bran-bread and cress or perhaps lettuce, with a stone mug of milk for the child when you could afford it. The London of that day had no luxuries for the poor. And having had none you missed none. But the populace lived in starveling misery. The rabble rose and rallied to the Gordon as it would have to anyone who urged it to rioting. You were Protestants but you regarded him as a weakling visionary. You watched the rioting in the streets with little fear, but the linen-draper and all other shop-keepers kept barred doors. You two were venturesome and were yourselves of the masses, and when the mob stormed Newgate prison you both stood watching with many other householders on the outskirts of the crowd, in terror but secretly half in sympathy. You were safe enough from the rioters who were intent on wrecking the gaol and freeing the inmates. It was characteristic of you as you were then to be out looking on at a murderous night scene with interest, carefully protecting the child from contact with the throngs."

Said I: "How long did that life last?"

Said the Soul: "Four years after that your sister changed from her bare little bed to a coffin and you went on alone achingly suffering her loss for long years. You lived to be seventy, a thin old woman, working latterly as one of the night nurses in a public hospital. You lived an abstemious outwardly self-sacrificing life and died alone, from hardened arteries, one autumn night."

Said I: "And was there an informing beauty for you, for you and for me, in my life then?"

Coldly said the Soul: "You were self-centered, for all your self-sacrifice. You reckoned it your duty to care for your sister. It was also your irresistible delight. And after her death you took self-satisfaction in self-sacrifice: smug - smug. For me there was a laming distortion in it all."

Said I: "Tell me some other life."

Said the Soul: "You were once a little thief in the streets of a later London. You picked pockets, you stole bits of food in Covent Garden market, you pilfered shop-tills, you systematically worked the wealthy throngs as they came from the Opera at midnight. You were known to the police as the cleverest child-thief in London."

It warmed my vanity to think of myself as clever in so theatric a rôle as thief.

Said I: "How did that life like you?"

Said the Soul, with a shrug of her delicate shoulders: "I had little to do with it and that in a negative way. My part in you was to keep up your heart in hungry hunted days. You were neither a good thing nor a bad thing: perishingly passive. And you were dead in a potter's field before your sixteenth birthday."

Said I: "How did the little Thief look?"

Said the Soul: "You were sufficiently ugly - an undersized form, a gamin face, bastard features."

Said I: "And I daresay ignorant?"

Said the Soul: "Ignorant of everything rated useful, but wise to the undersides of human nature and in the sordid viciousness of London slums. And singularly shrewd - what is called philosophical."

Said I: "Pray tell me another life."

Said the Soul: "An earlier time - Paris, some century before the Terror -

saw you a slim *fille-du-pavè*, a prostitute of a low cheap type, but with more brain, more of what is termed character than you have ever possessed. You had wit, will, *esprit*, determination. From having been at seventeen most obscenely of the streets you were at thirty a wonderfully grand courtesan: no better in what are called morals but possessed of very much inner and outer strength and luster. You were *chère-aimée* to men of brain, men of importance to the state, whose acts were shaded by your influence. And you achieved unusual wealth chiefly by the powers and strategies of your character. You lived in the extreme of luxury of that time and of your type - a delicate luxury, almost high-bred. You were wanton in amour, being physically extremely passionate, but admirably straightforward and strong in each matter and aspect of your life."

Said I: "You admired her?"

Said the Soul: "I was serene and vividly alive within you. You were in all ways, simply and completely, an honest woman, and for the only time."

Said I: "How could she be honest, since she lived by exchanging treasure of much personal economic value for cheap cheapest gold, trash, and a besmirched name: and all through two sorts of greed?"

Said the Soul: "You were honest since you made no pretense of any kind to yourself. You took no gold that you did not logically, humanly, or shamefully earn. You were consciously and unconsciously above all subterfuge. You wrought no ruin nor error nor darkness upon your own spirit or any other. You deceived neither yourself nor anyone about you. The tone of your life was of sun-shining simplicity and cleanness. There was no greed in you. You saw your way of life before you and lived it without degradation, with a positiveness of strength."

It is as if my Soul's view and mine were infinitely separate from being narrowly paralleled. The portrait was mystically familiar: but not by her light.

Said I: "Was she beautiful to look at?"

Said the Soul: "You were beautiful in a pallid saint-like French manner - an uncertain type of beauty which fatigue or depression turns to plainness. You had but little light charm of prettiness. But you had what counts for more than beauty: the nerve and verve of attractiveness, the force and fascination of physical being, the fragrance, the *flair* of the deeply-sexed woman. In one phase you were constantly preying and preyed upon, but with high valors of attack and endurance."

Said I: "Did she live in peace - had she no times of suffering?"

Said the Soul: "You had hours of violent bitter suffering. Paris has always accepted without countenancing the prosperous cocotte. And often you were infamously insulted at street-crossings by soldiers and *sergeants-de-*

ville as you drove out in your small bright-colored carriage. And you were hailed with opprobrious appropriate names by the ragged populace as they picked up silver pieces which you threw among them. Such things were stinging brands and lashes to you. But you bore yourself with entire courage. You gave much money to churches and charities but looked on such acts in yourself rightly as some slight weakness which would, however, be of benefit to the starving poor. I can not describe - so you could grasp it - the peace, the expansion, the freedom for me in that life and in that attitude."

The exact outlook of the Soul throws over me a veil of wistfulness, bewilderness, freedness, lostness which hides the material moorings of my life and casts me adrift on broad clouded seas.

Said I: "What was the end of that - how did she die?"

Said the Soul: "You died exquisitely, of syphilitic disorders. You were something past forty, badly broken - your looks were gone, your friends were gone, your money was not gone but it was of little use to you. But you smiled serenely and lived up personally and mentally to your smile. A surgeon and a fat mustached old woman saw you die in the beginning of that bodily rot - the just portion of the passionate whore - one sweet Spring dawn, with birds twittering in green branches outside your window and a great gold sun slowly breaking the mist. Then for once I left you with reluctance. I clung to you. The kiss of me was last on your fainting brain and your fast-cooling heart. For I was leaving, in an agony of my own, an *honest* person. And I knew not what might be my next petty prison."

Said I: "What was my next life?"

Said the Soul: "It was not so petty as were some others. You were next - about seventeen-fifty - a quaint extremely common little person. You were apprenticed as a child to a milliner in Liverpool, England. You grew out of that and became a dancer in a dingy theatre - a cheap bedraggled life. You were a cheap and bedraggled young woman. You wore odd gay tawdry frocks, hideous little shoes, ragged raveled silk hose, surprising bright bonnets. Your mind was a shallow pool filled with tales from shilling shockers and penny dreadfuls in which you believed implicitly. You were mentally degenerate, organically a fool, a wonderful snob. You wanted only wealth and place bitterly to deride and browbeat the low class to which you belonged - not from lack of heart but because you believed it to be the proper aristocratic manner. And what you wanted in mind you made up in temper. You quarreled, you came to blows, with your fellow-dancers in any of a half-score of small selfish daily disputes. Cleverness among you consisted in gaining any possible advantage over the others and in calling each other names. Also in maneuvering bits of money - as much as might be - from unpleasing men who hung about the dingy play-house. On holidays you were invariably half-drunk."

Said I: "And wherein was she not petty?"

Said the Soul: "You believed in yourself. You had not a doubt you belonged in worldly high places but were kept down by the malice and depravity of human nature, people about you. And you lived up to your vulgar ideal of ambition. There was a simplicity, an enlightening pathos in you then which was lacking in the linen-draper's lodger."

In my flawed way I saw that, but objected to the bygone Liverpool lady from many an angle.

Said I: "Had I no life of a sweetness and gentleness and with it something that buoyed and bore you on?"

Said the Soul: "Never once. You were many centuries ago a Greek girl of the aristocratic class, bred in an intellectual life. You read the philosophers in the cool retreats of an olive grove. The mental knowledge you have now compared to your learning then is a tangle of ignorance. But the Greek girl had no heart, no human flame, no active blood of personality. Those wanting I starved. The Liverpool dancer in her warming virile vulgarness bore me vastly farther on my way. You were a Greek woman in a still earlier time - of a type which murders all simplicity. Your body and mind were haunted by perfervid imagination and both ached with the weight of it. You were made of twisted fires. I grew in *that* day: grew burdenedly: grew distortedly."

Always those Greek visions are my "half-familiar ghosts." -

Said I: "Was I sometime a married woman?"

Said the Soul: "You were - in four separate ages. Which brought you and me singular solitude."

Said I: "Was I always woman?"

Said the Soul: "You were once a young lad of fierce temper and were at twenty a madman. And died mad. No male body and brain could withstand and outface merely the emotional besiegings of *you*."

Said I: "When I went mad, what of you?"

Said the Soul: "I fell asleep, and knew no rest, but dreamed."

Said I: "Of what?"

Said the Soul: "Things I always dreamed in your mad lapses - poetry served very conscious and very hot: the material Color of the Sunshine: the musical Softness of the Dawns: the pulsing Thoughts in Girls' Throats: the Scent of Water-Falls."

The Soul has an airless voice which tells her meanings, beside her words and in their rhythm.

Said I: "What do you, and how do you, with me now?"

Said the Soul: "I grow tired with you. Exasperated. Desperate. As if I too wore flesh. You are a deathly prison, a torture chamber. I turn everywhere and nowhere at all. You tire me - you wear me. I wait. I stay. Yet I move."

She looked lovely, my Soul - and quite in and of this bitter-ish lovely world in its bloody bitter wrappings of bone and flesh. Around her neck was the Necklace she wore in all the ages, showing greenish in a dusk of gentian blue. -

All of it slyly garbles and cross-purposes me a little bit more than usual.

I wish I'd been born a Wild Boar.

*

Not Quite Voilà-Tout

To-morrow

The clearest lights on persons are small salient personal facts and items about them and their ways of life.

To know that a woman is 'sensitive' is to have but a blurred conception of her as one easily impressed, easily hurt. But to know that she wears thick union-suitish under-clothes and uncompromising cotton stockings is to know much about her: by those tokens she is plain: she is stupid: she is smugly virtuous: she is poor: she is narrow-thoughted: she lacks imagination: she is prosaic: she has a defective sense of humor: she is catty: she is 'kind': she catches cold: she is a thoroughly good woman. To know that a child is 'bright' is to have no definite knowledge of the child. But to know she flies into rages and bites whisk-brooms, laces and her fragile grandmother is to have a wide-beamed far-reaching spirit-light upon her.

That I am 'thoughtful' means little or anything or nothing: that I love the odor of ink, that I hate the stings of conscience, that I never lounge untidily about the house or in my room but am always 'groomed,' those tell me to myself. Here for my enlightening I write a garbled list of my items and facts:

- I never see a soft new yeast-cake without wishing to squeeze it for the salubrious feeling of the tinfoil bursting facilely and the yeast oozing with its odd dry juiciness through my fingers.

- And I never see a shiny waxy green rubber plant without wanting to bite the leaves precisely and daintily with my sharp teeth.

- My luncheon each late midday is made of four radishes, three crackers, and a thin glass of water: an anchoretic feast which I eat with relish. The rhyme I murmur with it is: "what do you think, she lives upon nothing but victuals and drink."

- Whenever I look out my window at five in the afternoon I see a neat nice-looking strange black woman walking past. And the black woman glances casually up at my window and sees me. We are unknown to one another and have belike as much and no more in common as if we grew on different planets. But the black woman and I are someway dimly liking each other and dimly knowing it.

- I scent my belongings faintly with Houbigant's Quelques Violettes perfume.

- I like to light a box of matches at a twilight window-sill singly and by twos and threes and little bunches, and hold them till they burn out, and watch the little flames, and drop the burnt ends out the window: a pastime inherited from my child-self.

- Of living creatures that I know I most hate cockroaches.

- Of inanimate things that I know I most hate a loose shutter rattling at night in the wind.

- When I smoke after-dinner cigarettes downstairs I put flat round black records on a tall red Edison phonograph and I curl up in a leather chair in the dark to listen to the music which is soft and deep: "Che Gelida Manina" in a wistful tenor, and "Refrain Audacious Tar," and "Ah Quel Giorno," and "Scenes That are Brightest," and others and others - tantalizing, tawdry, artistic, cheaply pleasant, luring, whatnot. And by turns it makes me lighthearted, lightheaded, emotional, romantic, restless, evilly coarse. It is piquant debauchery. Music sweetly poisons me.

- My bureau-drawers I keep neatly in order - lingerie and other articles arranged convenient to my hand in white rows and fragrant tidy piles: with the exception of the upper left-hand drawer which is a bit of terrific snarled chaos. In it is an inky handkerchief of an old vintage: in it are several unmated crumpled gloves: in it are some olive-pits: in it is an empty sticky liquid cold-cream bottle with tufts of eider-down powder-puff stuck to it: in it is a tangle of smudged ribbons: in it are two pieces of pink rock-candy: in it is a spent yellow-silk garter: in it is a torn sponge: in it are blackened pieces of chamois-skin: in it is a broken scissors: in it are three twisted ragged black-net veils: in it is a brass curtain-ring: in it is a broken scattered string of coral beads: in it is a lump of wax: in it is a piece of knotted twine: in it are little bunches of cotton wool: in it is a spilled box of powder whitening everything: in it is a spilled box of matches: in it is a jet bracelet broken into small pieces: in it is a broken hand-mirror: in it are some crushed cigarettes: in it is a ruined blue plume: in it is a warped leather purse: in it is a damaged lump of red fingernail paste: in it is a stick of gum arabic: in it is a bisque kewpie defiled by wax, ink, paste, powder, and rock-candy: in it are some partly melted vestas: in it are other bits of rubbish: all in wildest disorder. Why I do not empty the drawer and burn the rubbish I don't at all know.

- I sometimes take one or two of the neighborhood children to a picture-show.

- Sometimes as I lean at my window I alternate looking at the distant deeply-blue mountains by looking at the near-by women who chance to pass on the stone pavement below - the smartly-clad and light-hearted-seeming ones. I look at their good shoulders in pastel-toned silk and at their trim silk ankles and proud flaring skirts and insolent beautiful hats - the buoyant worldly insouciance of their ensembles - as their owners walk along on happy errands. As I look I feel Me to be behind prison bars looking out in thin psychic jealousy: regret for a time when I also went thus buoyantly on happy worldly errands and an odd raging silent impatience for a time when I may again. But with it too the wavering acquiescence in this analytic-writing mood.

- "Pussy-cat-mieow," I ruminate, "can't have any milk until her best petticoat's mended with silk."

- One kind of man I impatiently scorn is the kind that looks bored if I mention Ibsen or ceramics or Aztec civilization but is interested instantly, alertly, if I mention my garters. Equally I abhor the type that begrudges me my own private phases of amorousness: not those who condemn me for them: not those who dislike them in me: not those who deplore them: but who *begrudge* me them.

- Always I come up a stairway softly. Always I close doors softly. I make no noise.

- The quaintest character I have met with in fiction is Huckleberry Finn's father, looked at as a father. Next in quaintness I place Sally Brass, regarded as a human being.

- I like a glass of very hot water and a dish of preserved damson plums on a sultry August day: and another of each on top of that: and another of each on top of that.

- I like the word addle: I hate the word redress. I would fain have my "wrongs" ever addled than redressed: merely for the word prejudice.

- I would rather that almost any physical disaster should befall me than that I ever achieve an "abdomen." When an abdomen comes in at the door life's romances fly fast out the windows: so it looks to me. May death overtake me haply before the menopause.

- The pictures I have crowded on a small side-wall space two feet from my eyes as I sit at my desk are: Theda Bara as Carmen: the late Queen Isabella of Spain: Marie Lloyd, loved of the London populace: a velvety-looking black-and-orange print of a leopard: Blanche Sweet, loveliest of film actors: John Keats, a small old print: Ethel Barrymore, a pencil drawing made by herself: Nell Gwyn, a photograph of a Lely portrait: Watts' "Hope": Stanley Ketchel, dead middle-weight fighter: "Jane Eyre" by a Polish artist: Fanny Brawn, the solitary extant silhouette print: Ty Cobb: two children: Charlotte Corday in the Prison de l'Abbaye: Susan B. Anthony: a Chinese lady: Andrea del Sarto: Queen Boudica: and Christy Mathewson.

- I am old-fashioned in many of my tastes - in all my reading and writing tastes. I do not like type-writers: they make fingertips callous in a poor cause. And I do not like fountain-pens which someway seem suitable only for business-letters, forgeries, book-keeping, and crude cursory love-letters. I like a steel pen in a fat glossy green enameled wood pen-holder with a thick pleasant-feeling rubber sheath at the lower end.

- I wear to-day a modest frock of black silk: beneath it a light silk petticoat: beneath that a white pussy-willow silk "envelope" and a pale narrow pink silk shirt chastened by many launderings: no stays: thick white silk stockings gartered above my knees by circles of mild mauve elastic: on my feet cross-ribboned bright-buckled black shoes: round my neck a jet necklace - all of it a costume that might be of a conventional woman, a plain-living woman, a good woman, a well-bred woman - saving only that beneath my left shoulder-blade the smooth new pussy-willow silk has a jagged two-inch rent where it caught on a drawer-handle: and the rent - in lieu of neatly mending it with the thread and needle of woman's custom - I caught up any way by its jagged edges and tied tight in a hard vicious heathen knot: the note of spiritual fornication, of Mary-Mac-Lane-ness: always there's some involuntary pagan touch to undo me, to arraign me, to betray me to God and to myself.

- I wear five-and-a-half A-last shoes: number twenty-one snug whalebone stays: and weigh a hundred-twenty-four pounds.

- I am fond of green peas, baseball, and diamond rings.

- I like violently to spoil a little charlotte-russe with a fork: it gives me the same feeling of lawless sweet-fiery lust which must belong to a Moslem soldier when deflowering a Christian virgin: and harms nobody.

- Sometimes when I'm dressing in the morning I glance down through my window and see two elderly Butte business men, one a lawyer and one a banker, going by on the way to their offices. And I wonder at how frightfully respectable they look in their tailored clothes and reproachless gloves and perfectly celestial-looking hats. I murmur: "Robin and Richard were two pretty men who lay in bed till the clock struck ten."

- I keep on my desk a little doll with fluffy skirts, blue eyes, pouting lips, and curly hair and named Little Jane Lee after an adorable child I have seen in moving pictures.

- I am five feet six inches tall in my highish heels.

- I wear number six gloves: the calf of my leg is a shapely thing.

- The six extant Americans I most admire are Thomas A. Edison, Harriet Monroe, Gertrude Atherton, Theodore Roosevelt, the remaining Wright Brother, and Amy Lowell.

- I think I'd learn to be a cook, a professional cook, if I were less easily fatigued.

- I love the sound of the clinking of two clean new white clay pipes, one upon the other.

- I crack nuts with my teeth.

Voilà!

But not quite *voilà-tout.*

*

A Damned Spider

To-morrow

To-day was one of the To-morrows of encompassing dissatisfaction when this seems all a nasty world and a nasty life.

A Spider drowned in my bath-tub this morning.

It was one of those long-legged spiders. It was in the tub when I went there - a small ovalish dark-gray pellet with seven ray-like legs as of an evil little sun lying flat on a white desert. It feels inconceivable that any creature should naturally have an odd number of legs: we are all, including spiders, laid out as with rule and compass. Perhaps it is inconceivable. But this Spider had seven legs. I counted them while I knelt, blue-peignoired, beside the tub with my elbows on the edge and watched the Spider and waited for it to go away. Whether it had lost a leg, or had one too many, or its kind is normally made like that: those things I vexedly wondered about. In either case it seemed a so much worse Spider. It did not go away so I touched it gently with an oblong of green soap. Then it moved and began to walk up the side of the tub. But the side is smooth as glass and always it slipped back. I went to my room and fetched a post-card.

With a post-card newly from Delaware I lifted the Spider out of the bath-tub. Then I scaled card and Spider to the farthest ceiling corner of the room. Then I drew the tub one-third full of tepid water. And there floating in it as if brought down by Black Art was the seven-legged Spider, drowned and ruined. It spoiled the atmosphere and anticipation of my morning tub. I shuddered miserably. I pulled out the rubber plug and water and Spider washed down and away into the dark sewer-wastes of Butte, into the bowels of the earth, through the gateways of hell, I hope. I took a hasty shower with a flavor of long-legged Spiders in it. I dressed, and combed and coifed my hair, with the clouded thought in me that throughout my life I shall inevitably encounter by eternal law a long-legged Spider from time to time. I know there'll be no evading it. Those who know statistics doubtless could tell me how many Spiders I shall encounter in so many or so many years: the exact percentage even to the division of a week and the half or the quarter of a Spider. There is something disconcerting and tragic in the thought.

The drowned Spider's ghost pursued me all day though its memory faded.

My breakfast, though it included an egg, seemed antagonistic, hostile toward me as I ate it. It made me melancholy.

I watched from my back window a slim boy painting a porch and singing in incipient tenor a rhythmic lullaby beginning "go to sleep my dus-ky ba-by." He painted silently for some minutes and then dipped his brush in the tin of paint. Whenever he left off painting to dip the brush he sang. Once he failed to sing when he dipped the brush but instead burst forth with it in the midst of painting a long mustard streak on his porch. Ordinarily that would not have mattered to me since I am innately keyed and pitched to expect the galvanically unexpected. But to-day it made me rackingly nervous.

In the afternoon I went for a walk. Down and down, seventeen squares from here, in a quiet neighborhood a strange woman accosted me. She was pale and smartly dressed and quite drunk. She said, "Listen - can you remember which of these corners I was to meet a friend at?" It made me feel annoyed and bewildered and sad and silly.

When I came back I read awhile - a story of Guy de Maupassant's about a little dog named Pierrot, whose owner loved him much but loved money more and could not bring herself to pay a tax of eight francs to make Pierrot's existence legal. So she threw him into a pit. As heartbreaking a tale as even de Maupassant ever wrote. It made all the loves in this world feel terrifyingly sordid. It made me unhappy.

Then I found a poetry-book and read about the Blessed Damozel leaning out from the gold bar of heaven. Always, by her loveliness alone, she stirs me to my still depths of tears. But to-day the song made me feel over-wrought and life-worn.

To-night I walked out to a little desert-space west of the town, a very pale, very gray desert, with a sweet wet mist like dissolving pearls swathing it.

The million placid stars looked down, remote and hard, as if each one had newly forsaken me. It made me afraid and cold around my heart.

Here I sit and nothing in all the world is pleasant and reassuring.

That damned Spider.

*

To Wander and Hang and Float About

To-morrow

My damnedest damningest quality is Wavering - Wavering -

I might say I prefer the dawn to the twilight or the twilight to the dawn. Neither would be true.

I love the dawn - I love the twilight.

What I unconsciously *prefer* is the long negative Wavering space-of-day between the two.

I might say I prefer heaven to hell or hell to heaven.

Neither would be true.

My garbled gyral nature, partaking uneasily of both, prefers to wander and hang and float about between the two.

I might say I prefer strength to weakness or weakness to strength.

Neither would be true.

What I prefer is a hellish hovering, an endless torturing Tenterhook between the two.

And that Wavering preference is against my will, against my reason, against my judgment, against my taste and liking - against my life, my welfare, my salvation: against the clear lights of my spirit.

I know I work intently and industriously at the articles of my damnation in the Wavering - Wavering -

I know it would be better to die at once: failing that, to live but to live positively as a beggar, a whore, a thief, or a milliner. Knowing that, I know also I Waver: I know I shall prefer to Waver: I know I shall constantly Waver.

I am constant - I am remarkably profoundly constant - in my Wavering.

In the morning as I dress I draw on a stocking - a long black or white glistening stocking. I know I do it only because the mixed big world, which refuses to Waver, is pushing - pushing me. I would choose if I could - though loathing my choice - to stay with my bare foot and my stocking in my hand, Wavering. Between drawing it on and pausing barefoot, Wavering. I prefer not to draw on the stocking: I prefer not to be barefoot: I prefer Wavering - Wavering -

When I'm hungry I choose: not to let food alone: not to eat it: to have it by me and Waver, Waver, emptily. Not to enjoy its anticipation: not to contemplate it. No - *no!* To *Waver!* I reach and take the food because the world in its pushing pushes me.

If the world stopped pushing -

One reason it will be pleasant to be dead: I can then no longer Waver.

Worms will eat me unwaveringly. Or they may then do the Wavering. But *I* shall no more pause with a bare foot and an empty stocking, a dish of food and a gnawing midriff.

Here I sit as yet, alive and Wavering.

The Wavering is not the pale cast of thought: it is not my way of analysis: it is only Wavering - Wavering -

Wavering is not among the blue-green Stones in my antique necklace: not by that name - not as one Stone.

It is a marked and hateful and hellish gift of this present Me who house my Soul.

It is half of this Mary MacLane - who is I -: and I know.

I am constant alone - noticeably tensely constant - in my Wavering: and less constant in Wavering than in the ghoulish preference.

An odd and subtle doom.

*

A Thousand Kisses

To-morrow

Among my other gifts I own also Wantonness. In proof of which I am wishing as I sit here for a Thousand careless kisses: eleven o'clock of still evening - a Thousand Kisses.

A wonderful, wonderful attribute, Wantonness: rich, rich luster in the conscious temperament which owns it, a Gift-thing delicate and gorgeous.

By it I want a Thousand Kisses: a Thousand - made all of Wantonness.

Kisses come in differing kinds and only one is Wanton.

The kiss of a lover has an intense cosmic use: the kiss of a mother is tender fostering food: the kiss of a friend is vantage and grace of friendliness: the kiss of a child is cool charm of snowflakes and green springtime leaves.

And the kiss of Wantonness is not of use, nor of food, nor of gracing vantage, nor of childhood charm - but is restless essence of humanness and worldliness and mere sheer limitless encompassing liking: born of sweet lips, alien it might be, and secretly "unattuned," but warm and fond and *present*: answering the pathos of infinite jejuneness which flows, flows always in red human blood.

Through the race rides a long dread wistfulness, made of tears and lies and the barbaric distress and pitfall of everyday's journey: a crying wish for a cup of warmed drugged sweet ease to turn it all a moment away: but a moment away.

And through all the race is the measureless poetry, purling and mantling in its bowl of flesh. Each human one is made of the sun, and made of the moon, and made of the four winds and the seas and the last pink sea-foam on the crests of the twilit waves: and made of salt and of sugar and of lonesome calling of loons and quick song of skylarks: and made of sword-edges and of money and of dolls and toys and painted glass: and made of loose reckless shuffling of dry autumn leaves, and of nerves and of illusions and of broken food and hesitance: and made of Mother-Goose rhymes and of cigarette-ashes and of raveled silk: and made of layers and layers of mixed-up passionate colors and of gilded cakes and of strawberries and of temperamental orgasms and raw silvery onions and gaming and dancing and minute-by-minute inconsistency: all veiled in a thin gold veil - all in a thin gold veil.

Betwixt the wistfulness and the poetry - *hélas*, what chance has the human equation, unsought, unwarned, unchallenged of God to be straitly equable!

No chance.

Happily no chance.

Thus I, Mary MacLane, so conscious of Me and garbledly gifted, want a Thousand Kisses at eleven o'clock of a still evening.

No spirit-hands of Love are laid soft on my drooping shoulders in the passing days: no Love - no Love - in all my life.

No miracle Wonder and Gentleness stirs in and against my Heart: my Heart is strangely dead of a strange Realness, known and felt but unachieved: - no Love - no Love in my life.

And I can wish for no Love, for the listless Heart is listlessly dead.

I wish instead, in hastening present clock-ticking moments, for a Thousand present-warmed Kisses: a Thousand in Wanton response to a Wanton 'leven o'clock.

Dominating waving washing warmth of Wantonness, compassing me at eleven o'clock.

A Thousand careless insouciant Kisses: a Thousand gorgeous delicate Kisses: a round Thousand.

From what lips - whose lips - what do I know? -: so their Kisses are a Thousand.

From what lips - what do I care? -: so they be eager and live and tenderly false.

- come some of the Thousand glowing on my pink lips, and my white fingers, which were tense, relax -
- come more of the Thousand, and my rigid hard-riding thoughts grow drowsy and pliant and negligible -
- come more of the Thousand, and my knees and the marrow in my bones are gently aware of most logical opiate ease -
- come more of the Thousand, and my midriff is full of cream-and-chocolate casualness and my smooth arms are washed down with mists of custom -
- come more of the Thousand, and my seven senses start to melt at the edges -
- come more of the Thousand, and the palms of my hands wax merely pleasant-feeling and the soles of my feet fatly comfortable -
- come the last of the Thousand in a swirling silly lovely lightly-insane shower - and I feel exactly like a woman in the next street who goes forth clad in mustard-and-cerise with a devilish black-and-white Valeska-Suratt parasol: and more - much more - I feel the way she looks -

For this Wanton-thing is not amour but psychology: in it I am less the mænad than the philosopher: less the Cyprian woman than the Muse.

I am a deeply gifted woman.

I am not prone on my green couch, frayed, frazzled, bowed-down in spirit from a day of frightful stress and cross-purpose.

Instead, hair-triggerishly alive, with definite desire beating hotly this moment in my throat: the wish for Kisses - Kisses far removed from Death and Graves and Coffins: Kisses of this present clock-tickingness, Kisses useless, meaningless, sweet - oh, *sweet!* -

- in number, a Thousand: in kind, Wanton.

*

A Fluttering-Moth Wish

To-morrow
A wish that God would come personally to see me flutters in my thoughts ever and anon like a restless moth.

I am in a prison-mood and coldly content to be in it. For how long content - content is not the word: despairingly acquiescent - there's no word to express that - I can noway tell. But now I live and breathe aloof and strange-mooded. And with it I wish God would visit me a moment.

It is not a strong wish. Yet restless and persistent. I want to be free from myself and away, loosed in the little broad big narrow World: but first and more I want God to visit me.

I want people again, those away from here who are my friends - some glowing-spirited ones who appreciate my Mind and cater to me: I want, I think, a poet to love me with some unobvious madness: but first and more I want God to visit me.

More than I want strength of spirit and flesh, more than I want a fat mental peace, more than I want to know John Keats in star-spaces: more than I want my dream-Child: I want God to visit me.

More than I wish this appalling tiredness would leave me: more than I wish this I write to be a realization, a *de-fait* portrait of the thin-hidden Me, my self-expression achieved: more than I want to be quit of my two black dresses and back in the wide sweet frivol of variegated clothes: I want God to visit me.

God must know all about that. He must have known it a long time. He still does not come.

If he would come and tell me one thing, one *certain* thing, it would be enough. It would show me a direction and I could keep on in it by myself. If God would tell me even a sheerest matter-of-fact, for *sure* - like What O'Clock by his time it really *is*: that would be a spark from which I could build an eternal fire for myself. Forever after I could dispense with God as a personality.

I am strangely weak. Strong of will, strong of mind, but weak of purpose: damnably, damnedly. I shall never be able to write in words one one-thousandth of the dramatic drastic weakness which is in me. But I hate weakness with so deep and strong a hatred, and to know one eternal certain thing would be so roundly restful, I could then go on: I could vanquish the potent pettinesses which beset me.

I do not want from God a passport, a safe-conduct into heaven. I don't want to get into heaven. I don't know what it is, but the word has sounds of finality, as if all winds, sweet nervous petal-laden winds, had stopped blowing forever. For cycles and centuries to come the Soul of me will be too restless to live where winds can not blow.

I love the journey: so that only I might have one dim torch to go by. I love the pitfalls and ditches - all the dangers - black-shaded woods and wolds, and lonesome plains and briery paths, and very wet swamps, and strong whistling gales which chill me: so that I could feel but one tiny bright-bladed truth, within and without, pricking and urging me to struggle on through it all till I might emerge at last like a human being, rather than linger indifferent and inanimate like a jaded wood-nymph in drearily pleasant spaces.

*

Twenty Inches of Ajarness

To-morrow

God might come to visit me on a Monday afternoon.

He would come in at the door of my blue-white room which had been left about twenty inches ajar: for I cannot imagine God, the aloof and reticent, opening a shut door to visit anyone.

It is as if God purposely lacks all initiative. If I wish to meet God I must first suffer deeps of terror and passion and loneliness to make the mood that wants it. Then I must train my life down to two plain frocks. And to crown all my room-door must be left ajar on the day he happens to come or he will not come in. That seems certain: but for twenty inches of ajarness at my door he will not come in.

In it God is quite fair. I do the reaching-out and I live out the despairs: he furnishes a fact to go upon: I go upon it, in some anguish doubtless: but then mine, not God's, are the lights and the translated splendor. It is a "gentleman's game" God plays. It is because I feel that to be true, more than for that he is the Dealer, that I would have a word with him.

On a Monday afternoon -

He might come in the figure of a precise mystic-looking little old man, punctilious of dress and manner like an English duke on the stage. He might wear overwhelmingly correct afternoon attire, with spats and a monocle on a wide ribbon. It someway fills my peculiar trivial concepts of God: mystic-seeming because he is the God of the dead dusty hosts of Israel, and punctiliously modern because he is also the God of new-poeted, radium-gifted Now. A God like a druid or like Aladdin's genie, such as I fancied as a child, or like Jove or Vulcan, would seem an inadequate and unsuitable God. What would such a one know of the shape and fashion of my two plain dresses, and of my shoes, and my breakfasts, and the charmed surface joy in the back of a magazine? God, to be God to me, must know all those things.

And if he only bespoke me in thunderous preludes touching souls' triumphant apotheoses - bold and intolerable ecstasies beyond heaven's last poignantest door - it would be nothing to my purpose. Those my poet-brain can make for me if I wish. But I'd like God to explain me the little frightful puzzles which thrive all around me in the wide daylight of this knife-and-fork-ness.

God might come walking lightly in and perhaps seat himself fastidiously in my chastest chair. He might cross one knee over the other. He might adjust his monocle and regard me through it speculatively or sadly or politely-wearily. I should be outwardly calm but I might feel an inward panic: lest he go away again without having told me a fact.

I might say to God: "God, if you please, this small blue vase on my window-sill - I see it and I touch it and I love it - will you tell me, you who *know*, is there a blue vase there or is there no vase?"

And God might merely glance at the vase through his glass and daintily hold his white handkerchief crumpled-up in his gray-gloved fingers and might merely say: "Madame, you have eyes with which to see the vase and hands with which to touch it and sentiments to lend it charm for you, no doubt. Then why not let them inform you as to its actuality?"

And then I might say, with a weariness equal to God's: "My senses are pleasant - they are sweet - but they do not inform me, or they inform me wrong. Because they don't plainly tell me whether it's a Blue Vase or a Blue Shadow - just for that I burn in little disconcerting hell-fires, and vulture-thoughts with beaks and talons come and tear me in the night, and I starve and decay trivially, and my life is a flattish ruin and a tasteless darkness and a slight shallow death, a death in the sunshine - I am fed-up with a sense of death because of pricking doubts as to my blue vase's realness."

To which, again, God might reply with his head tilted to one side, tranquil and impersonal: "As to that, Madame, there may be less death in doubt than in certainty about your vase. You might in discovering it discover in yourself no right whatever to the sunshine - no right to live in it, no right to die in it."

And I might answer, with some insolent feeling: "I should wish to discover the *fact* about it though it proved to me I don't exist and never existed - that I'm a dust on a moth's wing, and at that alien - not belonging there."

Upon which God, for what I know, might only shrug-the-shoulders.

In that identity he might shrug-the-shoulders or break-the-world with equal omnipotent plausibleness.

But I might try again. I might say: "One thing *feels* realer than my blue vase - this blue-and-green Necklace which my Soul wears. It is rare and recherché but my beautiful Soul is very tired from wearing it. Will you please unclasp it for me?"

And God might say, deprecatory: "Pray, Madame, do you consider what portion of the beauty you mention may be in the Necklace? Should I un-clasp it - it is doubtful whether you would recognize your soul without it."

To which I might answer, with more insolent feeling: "I don't know anything of that and I don't care for it. I only know I want the Necklace off. To wear it makes me languid and frenzied and worn - full of wild goaded saneness and the wish to go violently mad."

And God might answer: "Permit me to express my regrets for those senti-ments which, I should add, I neither concur in nor refute nor deny nor share."

There I might be: conversationally whip-sawed. -

God is full of works of beauty, serene and miraculous: Gray Lakes and Blue Mourning Mountains and Deserts beneath the Moon. Those have quietly ravished me many and many a night and day - and will again, and still again, in pacing To-morrows. But I can't tell What O'Clock it is by them. And if God were by me and I asked him the time the odds are all that he would look at the toy-face of my little ivory toy-clock, which sets on my desk where I can see it myself, and tell me the time by that. But though he is thus perplexing he knows the right time and could tell me it.

For that restlessly I wish God would make me one brief visit.

I wish that though he should so godlily baffle me and divinely bore me.

*

A Profoundly Delicious Idea

To-morrow

It is nineteen minutes after one on a summer night. And if only I felt a bit hungry this is what I should wish - spread out on a damask cloth before me in a few gold-medallioned Chinese dishes, with no forks or knives: first of all, two thin *foie-gras* sandwiches, four grilled snails, and maybe a little alligator pear: on top of those, two truffles: on top of those, two slim onions: on top of those, two thin salted biscuits: on top of those, a bit of Camembert cheese: on top of that, two cigarettes: on top of all a hollow-stemmed glass of sparkling Burgundy.

I'm not hungry, but it is comforting to think how delightful that supper would taste if I were. Food is a so magic rich gusty gift bestowed on the human race: and is besides a profoundly delicious Idea.

I like food better to imagine than even to eat. If I were hungry I think I could obtain that chaste supper item for item, and eat it: swallow it down magic and all, and thus vanquish it magic and all, and there an end. So I am glad I am not hungry. It is much more delectable to sit here and think that if I were -

- *if* I were -
- a Hollow-stemmed Glass of Sparkling Burgundy.
- two Cigarettes.
- a Bit of Camembert Cheese.
- two Thin Salted Biscuits.
- two Slim Onions.
- two Truffles.
- two Thin *Foie-Gras* Sandwiches: Four Grilled Snails: and maybe a Little Alligator Pear.

If I were a bit hungry: oh, the idea of a little supper! It would then be blestness, benediction - fruit of the very garden of Paradise!

*

A Mountebank's Cloak

To-morrow

I am so *Clever.* I am the Cleverest human being I know.

I have thought my Cleverness an outer quality, a mountebank's cloak, and as such not belonging in this book of my own self. But there are no outer qualities. Everything in and about me is my own self.

My Cleverness is of high quality - even supernatural, I have thought - and is of unobvious tenors.

To any essentially false nature, such as mine, a quick and positive Cleverness is its needfulest resource in coping with this pushing world. To any un-sanely sensitive nature such as mine Cleverness is its fender against human encounters and onslaughts.

There is no Cleverness in this I write. There is writing skill and my dead-feeling genius. But my Cleverness is beside those points.

I use Cleverness when I encounter people.

Sometimes I like people and wish to impress them.

Always I am vain and sometimes I wish my vanity catered to.

And I can get from people whatever tribute I choose.

I mostly choose to bewilder and half-fascinate, which is easiest: I talk about anything, nothing, everything with a tinsel-bright complexity which captures average intellects. And even very Clever people seem not Clever to me because I feel so exceeding Clever to myself. I am a little more intuitive, a little falser, a little lightning-quicker than the most artistically antic mentalities I have known.

I am a lady with the ladies, a woman with women, a highly intelligent writer with writers, a loosed fish with the loose fish: being all the time nothing but my own self, unspeakably incongruent. Having never found anyone remotely matching me in barbaric and devastating incongruity of nature I use in human encounters whatever phase makes the occasion most gently befit me. I cater, or I thrill some bastard dull brain, or I grow roundly versatile: all with a sudden coruscant Cleverness which is not in itself any of Me but is my mountebank's scarlet cloak.

But its main cause and reason is not vanity nor a fancy for piquant trickery, nor the wish to try my superior wings in glowing human atmospheres - the preponderant impulse to fly because I can fly. It's none of those, but a need of protection, of a bright armor to keep other people's superficialities from touching me. There's a human effluvium which I feel from people which would touch, wrap, enclose me in a harsh vapor - a half-froze, half-stinging worldly cloud. It hurts with thin cruelness like a corroding spray of acid on my skin: unless I send out the sudden air of my own Cleverness to keep it off and away.

It is long months since I have encountered people with any impulse save hastily to avoid them. But if I should meet, with an aggression of mettle and mood, some woman or man or little group of human sorts (except children of and for whom I have always a fear and a respect) I should then suddenly be casual and half-fascinating and phosphorescently glowing and insolent: being inside me haggard from solitude, wistful from a bereftness and a beauty-sense, suffering and lost.

Ah, I'm notably Clever!

I write a letter of Clever delicate surprisingness - it is the only Clever writing I do. There are twenty people, now long outside my life, to whom a Mary-Mac-Lane letter is the agreeably-vividest thing that could come into a day. The letter, which is an unapparent cater, is not real Me who am someway a strong and contemptuous spirit - but instead one tinsel facet. And it makes people - people! people! - admire and defer to me in a subtlest human aspect: an unwilling antagonistic homage. It stays me, buoys me for the time.

I am profoundly Clever in that I who am in reality so futile, so wavering, so sensitively lyingly artistic, can still show myself aggressively Clever to other persons. I must, being false, be Clever in order to get by.

It is at its best a trickster's quality: and so much the more am I Clever in stretching it out over my shaded life like a strong bright cloak-of-mail.

Just to be Mary MacLane - who am first of all my own *self*! - and get by with it - how I do that I can not quite make out.

I'm by odds the Cleverest human being I know: more than likely one of the Cleverest who ever lived in this world.

*

A Familiar Sharp Twist

To-morrow

I have - a Broken Heart -

It is nearly a year now.

It feels strange to be writing it. What *is* one's Heart? But it is a plain fact of me.

I have not had a Broken Heart in the years before. I have had silly fancies - I have wasted the outer tissues of my Heart, and it has been bruised and battered. But nothing pierced deep enough to break it till this.

My Broken Heart is the outstanding inner item of my life: and it still is a very small thing even in my own reckoning. It tortures me minutely all the minutes and moments and hours. And yet my all-round life moves on beside it and often passes it on the road.

My Broken Heart contributes nothing, no cause and no urge, to the writing of this song of my Soul and bones. It rather is a handicap. It makes me sit and brood. It makes my eyelids heavy and my head droop. It makes my shoulders ache. It makes me sit longish half-hours with my head on my lonely hands. It fills me with foolish wasting despair.

Its foolishness is the foremost thing about my Broken Heart. It is not a foolishness of worldly reasons nor of outer causes but of all the surprising folly of myself crowded into my Heart and into that which Broke it. The foolishness would not be so noticeable if the Brokenness were not so hideous and genuine and actual and matter-of-course. It was foolish to lay myself open, who am humanly starved, to the possible Breaking of my Heart: and doubly foolish to let it be Broken. And being left in possession of a Broken Heart I feel it to be a triply insanely foolish thing: but complete and absolute and natural.

I am so oddly a fool.

The proper price for such or such a thing in the Market might be one-and-twenty drops of red human blood. But I headlongly pay for it one-and-ninety drops: each one touched with fire, shot with purple, tinctured with hottest spirit-essence. The proper payment for Love is to pay back value received - which is enough. But I in addition dip my white bare foot into red world-and-hell flames by way of quixotic bonus. When other persons emerge from Love with the old-fashioned accustomed wounds and scars I emerge with besides an immensely useless futilely ruined foot.

It is wildest foolishness. Not merely folly. Folly is something picturesque - a bit romantic.

I am oddly a fool. It is that consciousness that rushes over me with each sad black thought of my Broken Heart.

My Broken Heart - it feels half-false to myself as I write it. And the written words look half-false to my eyes. But it is realer than my fingernails: than my palms: than my aching left foot.

My Broken Heart, besides being a triviality is a mistake, and will pass in time doubtless, but is long about it.

It is one thing I do not dwell upon in this book of me. A Broken Heart is sharply immediate like a newly-bitten tongue. It may bleed at a touch. To dwell on it connects me strainedly with the world around, and the world is really gone from me. This book is I as I breathe alone. I cannot write in it the silly shadowy Breaking of my Broken Heart. This writing is I Just Beneath My Skin. My Broken Heart is beneath bones and flesh. And though my M.-MacLane heart intact is wildly individual, my Broken Heart is merely human: made not alone by me and not alone by God. Its place in this I write is just outside the margins.

At times my Broken Heart feels far off while I'm feeling it hideous and wan inside my breast. Myself is Me, and much of Me had nothing to do with my Heart when it Broke: though I loved with all of Me, I loved with all of Me one who lives in New York - and I lost and lost, all the way. There was mere human ordinariness about which I built up a strangely sincere temple-of-grace which I looked to see shed light on my life like the new eternal beauty of a Day-break. I gave the best I knew to it, from the distance, and I lost. The day was a little day and broke at last only like my Heart. All was broken without so much as clasp-of-hands.

I am realest, strongest, passionately-sincerest in my essential known falseness -

It was all foolish and petty and someway false but I felt foolishly and shudderingly that I could live no more. But I am singularly brave from life-long custom. I have no pleas and surrenderings in me. I shudder but live on.

One Thursday I felt suddenly oppressed and beset and something in my throat cried out to the absent God to help me and guard me.

It was something in my throat which shrieked it dumbly in the deafening silence in my room. It was not I myself: for I am unsuppliant toward everyone human and divine though there often come such Thursdays.

Harder than Thursdays are Fridays and some other days when comes a familiar sharp twist beneath my chest-bones without the cognizance of my remembering thoughts: and when though I strive against it my Broken Heart makes me sit longish half-hours with my head on my hands.

*

A Dark Bright Fierce Fire

To-morrow

I am Lonely. I am so Lonely that I can feel myself rattle inside my life like one live seed in a hollow gourd.

I am on fire with Loneliness.

I am living this month alone in this house. The solitude is pregnant: Doors and Door-knobs and Curtains and Tables have silently come alive in it and have taken on identities like those of tamed wild beasts.

I do housework - I dust window-sills and water flowers. I gather up newspapers and brush the floors with a dust-mop. I wash my dishes. I cook my breakfasts. I look out of windows. I linger at screen-doors.

I answer the telephone: I say, "They're not at home."

I change my frock and put on a hat and a cloak and gloves and go softly out the door and front gate on an errand.

I meet people on the street whom I know, whom I may speak to, whom I may avoid: who may speak to me: who may avoid me: for I am at best well hated in this Butte.

I come back again, softly unlock the door, and come in. I come upstairs, take off the out-door things, give a hasty side-glance in my glass, and go downstairs.

I read awhile. To-day I read an old-fashioned short story whose soft wondrous prose cadences fed my senses - the Parable of the Prodigal Son. - for this my son was dead and is alive - was lost and is found -.

But I am very restless and cannot read long. I am on fire - dark bright fierce fire with Loneliness.

I move about again from room to room. I look out of windows and linger at doors.

I close my eyes and open my eyes.

My Soul-and-bones! I'm afire with Loneliness!

It is Loneliness not made of the Empty House and the tamed wild Door-knobs and Doors and Curtains and the Lonely Errands. Those are its small-fruits. Itself is my ancient daylight Loneliness dating from Three-Years-Old when I first began whisperingly analyzing things and finding little life-items to be of a fierce bitter importance.

If I were living among people, friendly people, then the Loneliness though unchanged would be disguised and vested with a padded muffling power - false, belike, and a mistake (but everything *is* false and a mistake: only there are wrong mistakes and right mistakes) - but made of the world-stuff that lets a human being get by in this nervous life.

But it would be of no use now. I must face Loneliness: and outface it. I do, and with no effort: for I am Lonelier than Loneliness' self. So it feels. This locked-in mood - soon it may be worn down and outgrown, and the husks blown away in the winds.

But may come after it a wilder Loneliness of being free, fearfully free: flavored with the heaviness of rain at night and draggledness of beggar-women's skirts. -

Meanwhile bright and black among Doors and Door-knobs and Curtains and Tables burns the fire of this Loneliness with strong, strong flame. It is mystic agony. There is no thinking in it. There is an utterly irrational wish, an aching yearning for people: not people to see, or listen to, or talk to, but - humanness I could *feel* with familiarity. I wish for hands and bodies near me: breath for mine faintly to mingle with: the feel of their human garments in the room around me: the feel of the pulsing blood in their veins remotely vibrant in the air: the feel of minds and spirits and throats and rich warm virile hair of human heads keeping me warmly company. I have heard one may step rarefied out of this living-place into the Fourth Dimension, where one feels everything without the efforts of feeling, and knows everything without the weights of knowing. It might be that I grope for in this black bright anguish.

Yet I feel rarely rarefied, heavily rarefied, wornly rarefied in this living-place where Loneliness burns me in strong fire and where I can shake my life like a hollow gourd and hear the eerie rattling sound I make in it.

*

Late Afternoon

To-morrow

Last night as I slept I dreamed a vivid dream.

I dreamed it was late afternoon and I was locked in a condemned cell, sentenced to die. I would be led out and hanged on a gallows the following morning at day-break. I dreamed I sat beneath a narrow window in the cell through which shone the light of the waning afternoon. The light was very pale, as of sunshine long dead. I dreamed I held on my knees a small block of paper which had a half-inch blue border at the top to mark a perforation, and in my hand I had a red pencil. And I dreamed I had cheated the gallows and was writing a little ballad about it in sudden rhymes and rhythms quite alien to my waking forms. When I awoke the song was still beating time in my brain. And with my black awake-time pencil I wrote, except for two words, the rhyme, title and all, as I dreamed:

Late Afternoon

They'll think when I pass through that door
To-morrow in the dawn,
I'll then be going to my death.
It's I've already gone.

They'll watch me walk serenely out,
Still-nerved and somber-eyed,
"So strong," they'll say, "to meet her death."
To-day it is I died.

There'll be my pulses quick with life,
My white sweet throat, my breath:
But flesh and bone are all will hang.
This noon I met my death.

For days I charmedly dwelt on death -
I raved at death - I swore -
Till vexedly death waived the date:
And came this Day-Before.

From being lured with artful thoughts
My life abortive grew.
From being broached in livid mood
My death aborted too.

To-morrow they'll remark my calm -
No fuss, no fright, no swoon.
They'll kill a wench to-morrow dawn
Was dead to-day at noon.

Three oddnesses are in that dream:

- that it is true to life in that I in my lightning Mary-Mac-Lane-ness *would* manage to cheat a gallows.

- that it is untrue to life in that instead of writing of it in the true twilit poetry of my own sufficient prose I wrote it in the shallow trick-phrasing of rhyme, a little serenade to the gibbet.

- that it catches and holds my Shadow-self who lives not *in*side me but *be*side me: the resembling dissembling shadow I cast when I stand between the daylights of the actual world and the quivering films of the region of dreams. -

My owned mysteries thrive apace. They are poetry and beauty and loveliness yet they bruise and batter me and split me to atoms. Withal are terrifyingly superfluous: they violently kill the wench to-morrow dawn who died restfully to-day at noon.

*

An Ancient Witch-Light

To-morrow

Also I am someway the Lesbian woman.

It is but one phase - one which slightly touches each other phase I own. And in it I am poetic and imaginative and worldly and amorous and gentle and true and strong and weak and ardent and shy and sensitive and generous and morbid and sweet and fine and false.

The Lesbian sex-strain as an effect is reckoned a pre-natal influence - and, as I conceive, it comes also of conglomerate incarnations and their reactions and flare-backs. Of some thus bestowed it makes strange hard highly emotional indefinably vicious women, turbulent and brilliant of mind, mystically overborne, overwrought of heart. They are marvels of perverse barbaric energy. They make with men varied flinty friendships, but to each other they are friends, lovers, victims, preyers, masters, slaves: the flawed fruits of one oblique sex-inherence.

Except two breeds - the stupid and the narrowly feline - all women have a touch of the Lesbian: an assertion all good non-analytic creatures refute with horror, but quite true: there is always the poignant intensive personal taste, the *flair* of inner-sex, in the tenderest friendships of women.

For myself, there is no vice in my Lesbian vein. I am too personally fastidious, too temperamentally dishonest, too eerily wavering to walk in direct repellent roads of vice even in freest moods. There is instead a pleasant degeneracy of attitude more debauching to my spirit than any mere trivial *trainant* vice would be. And a fascination in it tempers my humanness with an evil-feeling power.

I have lightly kissed and been kissed by Lesbian lips in a way which filled my throat with a sudden subtle pagan blood-flavored wistfulness, ruinous and contraband: breath of bewildering demoniac winds smothering mine.

Lesbian essence is of mental quality. There are aggressively endowed women whose minds are so bent that they instinctively nurture any element in themselves which is blighting and ill-omened and calamitous in effect. There are some to which the natural inhibition of their own sex is lure and challenge. There are some so solitary by destiny and growth that the first woman-friend who comes into their adolescence with sympathy and understanding wins a passionate Lesbian adoration the deeper for being unrealized. There are some so roiledly giftedly incongruous in trait that they are prone to catch and hold any additional twisted shreds afloat in human air-currents.

Each of those influences biases the Mind of me, which is none the less a clear-visioned mind which rates no thing a truth which it knows to be a lie: though it batten on the lie.

- often here and there around this human world the twisted and perverted and strongly false concepts are the strong actual working facts and the straight road is myth - myth - existent but in visions -

I don't understand why it's so: I know it is so.

Not only so with me: so with millions whose stars jangled.

Not always. But often. -

The deep-dyed Lesbian woman is a creature whose sensibilities are over-balanced: whose imagination moves on mad low-flying wings: whose brain is good: whose predilections are warped: who lives always in unrest: whose inner walls are streaked with garish heathen pigments: whose copious love-instincts are an odd mixture of mirth, malice, and *luxure*.

Its effects in me who am straight-made in nothing, but strongly crooked, is to vivify tenfold or a hundredfold or a thousandfold in my shaded vision the womanness of any woman whose inner or outer beauty arrests and stirs my spirit.

I see in some woman, some girl, any who attracts me - be she a casual acquaintance, or a Victorian poet dead fifty years whose poetry and portrait live, or an actor in a play, or a sweet-browed friend, or an Old Master - I see one such as if all her charm were newly painted and placed near me shining wet with delicate fresh paint. It is bewitching to look at: it has a deep seductive fragrance of smell: it is luxuriantly aromatic to all my known senses - and two senses unknown float from my deeps and rise at it. The Stranger becomes a dearly poignant fancy to dream over. My Friend turns into a vivid goddess whose fingers and hair I would touch tenderly with my lips.

Because of it a little flame, pale but primal, leaps from the flattest details of life. In such a mood-adventure a window-shutter blooms: a hair-brush glows: a sordid floor has gleams upon it. These bewildering frightful beautifulnesses in this life -.

- withal the same inherence which makes me someway Lesbian makes me the floor of the setting sun - strewn with overflowing gold and green vases of Fire and Turquoise - a sly and piercing annihilation-of-beauty, wonderful devastating to feel - oh, blighting breaking to feel - oh, deathly lovely to feel! -

It is the bewitched obliquities that run away with me: grind, gnaw, eat my true human heart like bright potent vitriol.

What God means me to do with such gifts and phases - I don't and don't understand. I never get anywhere as I think it out. I don't know shades of rights and wrongs since that ancient witch-light has found more trueness of human feeling in me than has any simplicity my life knows.

It began, they say, with Sappho and her dreaming students in the long-ago vales of Lesbos. It may be, I daresay. I know it did not stop there. And I know that - Greek, French, Scotch, Italian - Welsh - Japanese - *all* women sense its light lyric touch.

For myself, I only know it is part and parcel in my tangled tired coil.

I don't know whether I am good and sweet in it or evil and untoward.

And I don't care.

*

The Gray-Purple

To-morrow

Close at the east edge of this Butte is a barren ridge of Rockies that is sudden and big and breathing-looking, barbarously personal, touched with varying gifted color-moods and glowering morose color-passions: at the south the snow-topped Highlands lie long faëry solitary miles away, caressed at their summits by thin soft sun-rings and sun-vapors of salmon and sea-green and turquoise and mauve: at the west a gray-shadowed desert burns red-gold in the setting sun and sleeps in pearl-and-ashen stillness under midnight stars: at the north smaller spurs of the range break into foothills and bluffs and gulches, restful wastes of lonely stones and blurred radiances of tawny sand: on top of all the rarefied air of these plateau heights refracts the light into hot dazzling prisms at any vagrant flash of sun on a trailing storm-fringe. This Butte is capriciously decorated with sweet brilliant metallic orgies of color at any time, all times, as if by whims of pagan gods lightly drunk and lightly mad.

St. Paul-Minnesota looks a greenlier-prettier town: the Arizona Cañon looks vastly more fearfully beautiful: Wichita-Kansas probably looks more a regular town: Akron-Ohio doubtless looks more Americanly reassuring: Rome-Italy must have a more "settled" look: New York is much larger and much brighter-looking.

Only this Butte looks deeply and exactly like Butte-Montana.

Its insistent charm is that it goes on strongly resembling itself year after year.

There is love in me for this Butte.

I am profoundly lonely in it: my life-tissues are long familiar with the feel of it: its mournful beauty has entered like thin punishing iron into my Soul: and my love for it is made of those things. For no *reason* I feel love for this Butte.

As much as for the mountains in their mourning intimateness I feel love for all the outsides and surfaces of the town itself: the stone streets full of houses and shops and stores and brick walls and laundry-wagons and persons: the vacant lots where boys play ball: the school-buildings which for twenty years have needed the same green grass around them and the same playgrounds for schoolchildren to play in (and will go on twenty years needing them): the little mines in unexpected mid-town blocks with their engines and hoists and scaffolds and green coppery dumps: the big mines on the Hill busily working day and night, a bristling citadel of smoke-stacks and tall buildings above the treasure-drifts and tunnels that come down honeycombing the town under its streets and houses and yield up wealths of monthly millions: the desolate wind-swept cemetery on the Flat: the Timber Butte: the School of Mines: the Brophy grocery-window full of attractive grocery-food: the St. Gaudens statue of Marcus Daly: the few sweet green trees on North Montana Street by the court-house: the edge of Walkerville: Ex-Senator Clark's old-fashioned closed house in Granite Street: the stone Episcopal Church with the memorial windows: the surprising steep Idaho Street hill: the old Reduction Works reminiscent of the bygone Heinze and the bold buccaneering days: the Montana Street cemetery at last kempt and nurtured green as Beloit-Wisconsin: the little rocky Missoula gulch: the North Excelsior Street neighborhood where I wrote my Devil and Gray-dawn book: the Butte High School where I studied and meditated youngly: the old Library where I used to get a variety of books in my gangling girlhood: the electric ore-trains going to Anaconda: the vegetable Chinamen: the Post-Office News-stand: the Mexican tamale venders in the early night: the sweet green trees and other greenness in people's yards garnered and cherished in a way which would astonish Toledo-Ohio: the brilliant spar-kling look of the town from far out on the Flat late in the evening, like a mammoth broken tiara of starry diamonds, twinkling points of blue and orange and cerise and violet, fired and flung against a mountainside of dark velvet, - an aspect intensely Butte: the cool mosquitoless summer nights: the *Anaconda Standard*: the sulphurous smoky deadly-cold winter morn-ings: the Cornish and Irish and Austrian and Finn miners: the little slim green onions in the markets: the noise and color and morale of the crowds on a Miner's Union day: the markets on the afternoon shade side of West Park Street full of crabs and lobsters from Seattle and shining fish from California, and mushrooms and froglegs and squabs and hothouse things from hereabouts: the Parrot smelter: the Chinese gardens at Nine Mile: the Italian village of Meaderville: the fortified battlemented look of the town at the east of South Butte: the mystic familiar sand-and-barrenness -

All of it has a feel of something aloof and metallic and distinctive and gray-purple and Butte-Montana.

Gray-purple is the color of the town, its spirit-tone. Its odor and fascina-tion are gray-purple.

This Butte is bodily a young rich present-day city of a hundred thousand population, all told: miners who bulwark its foundations: masses who make and manage its business: millionaire-members who spend most of their lives and dollars in New York: all are Butte-made. But its soul is still the soul of the frontier mining-camp which sprang into copper being when the Comstock mine in Virginia-Nevada failed of its silver-ish promise.

A very few years ago - what one could count on one hand's fingers - there were no lids on in this Butte. Every summer bony thoroughbred horses from Juarez and Denver raced round the oval track on the Flat, watched by a shrieking betting throng of Butte citizens and citizenesses, ridden by silk-bloused black-booted jockeys, their finish-spurts under the wire chaperoned by a flock of book-makers. Roulette and poker and faro were wide-open in the town and flavored the air with a taste of gray-purple hazard. Gin-palaces and mining-camp dance-halls, highly de-luxe'd, lent their tinted breath to the current. Noodle-ish and little bacchanalian dives flourished in unexpected nooks. The police court on a Monday morning resembled the debris from an alcoholic human volcano, a condemned but owned portion of this Butte in its Butte-Montana-ness. All of it was but one element in an isolated prosperous town of many elements, but it someway tinctured all.

No pagan-wild sunset burst above the west desert but suggested that the vague lid was off the town, and vaguely lost: a lost lid.

The gambling lid is fast on now - if they gamble they gamble under it. And no more do ribby horses and surprising-mixed crowds disport them at the deserted race-track.

But the setting Butte sun suggests the same wealth and wildness as if always its celestial chemistry were shot with essence of mining-camp: rich, generous, feverish, and virile.

Brophy's grocery-window and the Marcus Daly monument and the Parrot smelter and the Clark house and the Idaho Street hill - all of it - owns the gray-purple which is not St. Paul and not Wichita and not Pittsburgh and not Spokane: not anything except intensely Butte-Montana.

I have felt it since I first lived here in little young short-frocked days, and I felt it when I lived away from Butte: I feel it all these now-days to the roots of myself.

I have no reason: but the contrary: to love Butte as a townful of human beings.

I have no friends in it, no feel-of-friendship, no human friendliness.

And the sculpturesque poetry of the outlying deserts and buttes pushes and presses hurtingly upon the lonely and introspective gazer in Body and Soul: I knew it as child and girl and woman.

There is nothing benign, nothing enlightening - no gentleness, no pity - in its barren beauty. But its hard chaste influence on the sensitive spirit is beyond any analytic power to gauge.

Its wonderful Aridness starves human nerve-soil till the sad wide eyes of the Soul grow bright - fever-bright, light-bright, star-bright - from denial and unconscious prayer: involuntary worship: homage of the unsuppliant unhoping devotee.

Because of that - and because of all its long-familiar outsidenesses - mournful, beautiful, mystic, lavish, madly-mixed, gray-purple - a fascination beyond plaisance or pain - I feel love for this Butte.

*

The Subdivided Cell

To-morrow

When I was twenty I was one strong Cell firmly, primly closing many little cells different from each other but each greenly intact.

When I was thirty the Cell had burst in dusty worldly winds and loosed the little cells. Those in turn had subdivided, losing strength by the cellful but gaining in shadowed truth by a roundabout road. And they showed me my fates and inevitablenesses as in a broad wrecked field misty but plain to view. And thus I see me in the subdivided cells:

- a piece of a normal woman.
- a piece of a child.
- a piece of a poet.
- a piece of a Lesbian woman.
- a piece of a writer.
- a piece of a jester.
- a piece of a savage.
- a piece of something someway brave.
- a piece of a student.
- a patriotic American.
- a lump of tiredness.

My strength is in knowing the evil from the good and the false from the true in it.

My weakness is in wildly waveringly inclining toward the false.

Except for love of my country I am ardenter, determinder, stronger in my falseness than in any of my shadowy truth.

*

Food and Fire

To-morrow

The first beauty in my life is John Keats.

In John Keats is my faith in some resurrection.

Without John Keats human nature feels to be something broken, menacing, unspeakably despicable and lost - lost in the shade. With John Keats the lights break across it and reflect the blazing yellow sun again from eyes and foreheads and fingers and shining hair.

There are world-and-human things which it thrills me to think about and dwell on: Nathan Hale on the British gallows: the charge of Pickett's Confederate infantry at Gettysburg: Henry V, prince among kings and men, at Agincourt: Charlotte Corday in prison: Columbus with his felon crews sailing westward: Susan B. Anthony - a woman made in a strange still heroic splendor half-incredible: Alexander Hamilton: Arnold Winkelried: the sea-worn Pilgrim women disembarking into bitter Novemberness.

Those thrill me because they are brave persons and brave things full of idealistic terrific strife: but they still are made of very struggling-garbled world-stuff - they are mere human fabric - till I think of John Keats: and at once they grow informing and eternal.

In his light the detailed world burns and glows!

John Keats! John Keats!

Other poets have written Nightingales and Grecian Urns and Sonnets and Mirth-and-Passion things: but *he* wrote them in his glorious and wistful pain. He wrote the sweet headaches of his spirit into his delicate beaten-gold verse: the precious fevers of his mental veins: the bone-aches and muscle-aches of his thoughts: the darling skin-damps and palm-damps of his divine fancy: - all in the Song of his lilied youth.

There is no poet but writes his poetry out of inner travails and immense wistfulness. But they all write just beside their travail, not in it: just beside their wistfulness, not with it. A poet who feels the throat of his soul aching and swollen and inflamed writes - not just that astral diphtheria, not till another time: but instead the fine smothering of a hope, perhaps, the oblique suffocating of a love. A poet whose brain-hands throb with some horrible dulcet-ish tiredness from handling the heavy bright tools of his craft writes instead the throbbing of his brain-soles and brain-insteps from walking small odd hard rutted daily ways.

It rouses me - it heats my eyeballs with salty honeyed warmth as I read: but it is not John Keats: who writes his own immediate magic sickness in perfect sudden obvious blood-warm golden *Now!*

It is always old, old-fashioned ailment, worn of ages. The drowsy ache of the Nightingale goes a thousand years back and a thousand years to come: the restless ecstasy of a thousand thousand Nightingales, one for each who reads, in any age, all ages. Long, long after the jeweled English language is gone, dead as Homer's, Keats' Nightingale will flutter lyric-winged in the nervous jeweled lovely *Now.*

"Weep for Adonais," wailed the differently-lovely Shelley, "he is dead." But he isn't dead. He is terribly living, passionately living.

Each day of my life I feel him living. He breathes. He breathes close to me, pantingly, like a swimmer breasting waves or a playing child in a summer day. - John Keats!

Just Beneath My Skin he is my God-of-the-World, my Fetich, and my Lover. He has been my Lover for seven gold years.

He is the first beauty in my flawed futile life. He is the most beautiful thing in the living and dying world. John Keats - John Keats! -

In everyone else I can feel mixed motives, tough tangled silk threads of self woven into wonderful wefts of days and deeds: in *everybody*, from Iscariot to Toussaint l'Ouverture, from Jeanne d'Arc to Victoria Woodhull, from Paul of Tarsus to Aaron Burr.

Only John Keats stands out alone, a true-breathing Poet, an Inmost Heart bleeding outward.

The lyric poet is the true poet. The lyric poet achieves no end in his art. He turns fragments of light and life into terms of beauty and sends them flying forth on flaming word-wings which translate the smooth human flesh they brush-by into delicious flesh-of-gold, flesh-of-petals, flesh-of-fire! But he makes no morals, teaches no lessons, finishes nothing. It's as it should be. Nothing *is* finished. The mixed world is all unfinished, a glorified Mistake. The race is a millionfold Mistake: lives it, breathes it, battens on it - coarsely and finely and lamentably and musically and bravely. So that all poetry which wanders from the lyric is only a play or a picture or an airship or a cause which aims at *fait-accompli*, attaining an object: it is limited and man-made: its beauty is lopped off like boughs and branches after a storm: its wings are clipped. Its distanceless spaces, little and large, are visibly engineered by mathematic hands. But the lyric poetry is the true luminous and bloody interpreting of humanness.

John Keats wrote by the lights of his living and he lived all his days in joyous lyric anguish.

Once he wrote, "Ever let the Fancy roam, Pleasure never is at home." It is a factful of himself - lawless, radical, and non-civilized, agleam in the mixed world. It is everybody - poets, burglars, nurse-maids: everybody. He wrote it in a hundred other ways, but it is all in that: it is the lyric epitome of every day. Pleasure never *is* at home.

And "Heard melodies are sweet," he wrote, "but those unheard are sweeter -"

There spoke the wild delicate wiseness of his brain and the passionate delicate wonder of his heart. - John Keats! John Keats!

But everything he wrote, the Grecian Urn itself, is immeasurably less lyric than himself writing it and being it.

He is rich bright-wet living lyric for this Me in this Now though he has lain dead in Rome nearly the full hundred years.

My garbled life and my thinking hunger feed upon him.

He was the one human one who walked on in the way before him: not around the jagged little stones and icy little pools that were in it: but straight on through them all, though his lyric feet were quivering shuddering sensitive, sensitive beyond knowledge of commoner feet that walk around.

It fattens my leanest self to keep that in my constant remembrance.

The thought of his brave radiant loveliness reassures me to myself, by the hour.

I am futile: but *he* is mysteriously omnipotently useful and I catch some of it from him.

I am half-full of vanity: but he is of a lustrous priceless vanity himself that justifies mine and all the world's.

I am fearing and false: but he is so brave, so true to infinite form, that by it he leavens the lump of the whole world's mendacious cowardice.

My brain is full of wilding darknesses, snarled and knotted gifts and penchants: but into *his* strong brain the strong fresh yellow rain-washed sun shines straight down - through the wide twin-brightness of his Eyes. I look down his Eyes - twin public wells (he belongs publicly and privately to all this mixed mad world, and anyone may look! -) - I look into that titanic vibrant brain, and mine catches some of it: a blest and precious Disease, oh, a rare Disease!

My Heart - my Heart feels strange and tired and dead, a bit of dead-sea fruit: but his heart, warm and real and boundlessly unsatisfied, is always the deep quick fragrant Rose of this World.

A Hero! - a Poet-at-arms! - John Keats!

"He has outsoared the shadow of our night," wrote that Shelley, and wrote no truer word.

I have read so many of the strange and splendid things - bits of them: Virgil and Homer and Villon and Goethe and all the English poets, and prose writers like Carlyle who in places out-poet poets, - and moderner ones and the new poets, imagists and others: John Keats feels a noticeably braver thing, and always, always a little way beyond. He is purely lyric.

When he loved a woman he loved the dubious fascinating Fanny Brawn - sordid-brained, worldly: to him a mixed living devilish-glowing goddess. A higher-souled woman would neither have so tortured nor so held him. He was purely lyric. He cared truly nothing for the verdicts of critics and reviewers: and in the sweet-lipped boyish beauty of his youth they truly and easily killed him. It would be like that - it had to be. He was so purely lyric.

He died in the sweet fierce dazzling cause of Beauty.

I have so many thoughts and my thoughts are always my own. There are endless written thoughts deeper than mine - finer, stronger, anything-you-like. But mine answer for me: no written thoughts affect them, though they thrill my reading hours. Only John Keats' thoughts can enter in and crush and cripple mine.

Because everybody is a little bit like John Keats I have a starry thin edge of faith inside me. He is food for my hunger of thought, fire for my passion of life. - John Keats!

He is the resurrection and the life. -

From my desk he gazes at me in a frame of old-gold. Every day the sunset on the glass blurs his large mournful joyous eyes with strangest agonized sunset tears: he shows me the sweet, sweet intoxication of his lyric grief.

He died young, unfinished - and oh, but it's a shivering ecstasy to think of all those lyrics in him he never wrote! - the sweeter melodies - "Unheard."

*

The Edge of Mist-and-Silver

To-morrow

Hidden somewhere in the invisible unused air-plateaus is a little Child: mine: who has never been born.

A tenet in me is that a woman by every right and by old earthen law should, if she will, have her child - should be the warm-winged mother.

I am a devil and a fantasy, a jezebel and a wanderer in fields of inverted fungi: so I seem to me. I do not know my status - I but know my personal incidents as they happen. But I am also woman: a woman by inherence and by fact. Being woman I am the potential mother, mother of my Child who has not been born.

I feel myself a fitting mother.

I am bodily in good health - if not robust yet durable, as a mother should be: I am always tired as if from touches and weights of living as a loving mother should be: I am warm of blood, latently savage-toothed like a jungle-mother, deadlier than the male, as a brave mother should be. Though I have no child I have an ancient right in my Child, and I want my Child. My Child *is*, but has not been, born. Merely to want my Child makes me a fitting mother.

My Child often is realer to me than books I read and walks I take and the friend who writes me frequent letters.

Sometimes my Child is a soft pink baby smelling of rain-water, milk, and flowers: lying close to the curves of my breasts in the hollow of my arms: feeding soft insistent baby hunger and feeding soft strong living hunger of my kissing mother-lips -

More often my Child is a little happy-voiced fellow, my small brave boy three years old: he clings to my skirt with his sweet tiny hand as we hurry along a frosty pavement in an early December morning. We live in New York in a little common quiet apartment and are gratefully poor, and I work in a factory for a little weekly wage for the living of my little fellow and me. Every day in the early morning we go out to a corner bakery to buy a long crisp loaf of French bread for breakfast. And in the December morning my heart contracts with a sort of happiness and a sort of grief at the sound of little feet in stout shoes yet frail shoes pattering-pattering gaily along beside me on the frosty flagstones. We start out hand-in-hand - his small hand is wonderfully firm and virile - but presently I let go his hand as we hurry along, to feel it instantly clutch the folds of my work-skirt: it pulls and drags at my waistbands and my Heart together with twisted sweetness that makes me ache from head to foot. "Mother, wait" he says in his happy voice, "wait for me." But I hurry faster. Always I hurry faster when my happy brave little fellow cries "Wait, mother," for the sweet feel of that dragging at my mother-skirt -

More often my Child is the little girl six years old of the shy eyes and the sun-kissed hair and the firm child-mouth, full of high temper and strong will. All over her is need and demand of her mother to guard and adore and cherish her every moment of her life. We are together in a country field with oak-trees in it, and poplars, and daisies and bluebells and other field-flowers, and it is overgrown with long coarse fragrant wild grass. The noonday sun is bright-hot and I bring my Child there to dry her hair, for I have newly washed it with a square of white soap and a porcelain bluebird bowl: the feel of her small round wilful head was marvelously fulfilling in my cupped hands. She wanders around in the hot-brightness through the tall grass, gathering the hardy scentless field-flowers with her little brown fingers, and she shakes back her beautiful thick short damp curls. I sit on a flat stone like a Sioux squaw and watch her. The grass brushes her bare legs: the magic sun mixed with a faint cool breeze plays upon her head: the tragic delicate music of rustling poplar leaves comes down from tree-tops and catches her in a fairy song-net. She is always very new, very incredible, my Child. She looks toward me with her shy radiant eyes and she says, "Mother, look, my hair is nearly dry." Her hair is thick and heavy. In my experienced subdued mother-wisdom I know it will not be dry for an hour. I feel the damp of her hair rheumishly keen all over me: a menacingness for me to guard her from: a dear anxiety: an ancient mother-note in the long human gamut of sounds.

- it is precious wearing racking colorful romance to be her mother: each mother-day holds gold-and-blue foreboding: each mother-day holds thin insistent gold-and-purple sorrows: each mother-day holds deep gold-and-gray care, incessant and absolute: an aching wealth of beauty: no more but no less than the damp of

her hair in the noonday field. My Child! - herself incessant and absolute: warm pure palpitant gold-of-my-life -

Someway realer than books I read and walks I take my Child clamors to be born.

My Child will never be born to any other woman. While she hovers and flutters on the edge of Mist-and-Silver - a border edge - there are ten million fertile hot milk-teeming bodies of women each ready to gather her in and wrap her in delicate-sweet flesh. Ten million other children hovering on the edge will drop off into the ten million matrix-cups - each woman mysteriously a fitting mother so only she wants her baby - though she be, besides, a thief or a traitor or a weakling or a murderer or a harlot or a drunkard or a fool.

Let them come, the ten million. The chrysalid children are clamoring, clamoring always for their birth: a wide "melody unheard."

But my Child will never drop over the edge to any woman but me. She calls with veiled and dazzling flames of eagerness for her Birthday: but she will await my made-readiness through a long night, though it should last till the day-break of another age. Dimly I weep for her, my needing-me Child. I weep that she must come to this richly-cursed me. But I weep more that I have not got her in this sterile now, where is flawed passionate wealth of intangible life-stuff: but no small round wilful head of hair to wash: no little fellow's feet on December flagstones and sweet dragging at my skirt: no soft pink baby hunger -

It is hunger I feel from her. I feel her always *hungry* where she is and I can give her no nourishing - no warming *food* in all my strange unfertile passing life!

It is that less than my empty arms that makes blurred unrests and writhing in my Dreaming Womb.

*

A Right Shape and Size

To-morrow

Sometimes I fancy me married - a responsible wife, a housekeeping matron: with my window-sills full of potted plants.

I have a woman quality which seems uxoresque: I am someway a Right Shape and Size to be somebody's wife. My bodily and astral dimensions have outlines apparently suitable for something in the married-woman way.

The wild piquance of being myself - who but for extreme saneness would be mad - rises up and smashes that concept.

But being a Right Shape and Size I involuntarily imagine it.

Fleetingly I imagine a flat in the West Seventies in New York, or a bungalow on the Jersey side, or a middle-sized house in a middle-sized town in Middle-West Illinois - whichever might happen - with me set marriedly down in the midst of it like a suitable maggot in a suitable nut. Suitableness, diametrically opposed to Romance, is its keynote.

I fancy me walking about my married house mornings after breakfast in a neat linen dress and high-heeled satin slippers: snipping dead leaves off my window-sill plants, dusting bits of porcelain, giving my maid some tame household directions. My Body looks slender and supple and newly-married and in-the-drawing in the linen house-dress. The geometric gods regard me with immense satisfaction as being an exact proved theorem. I go to the telephone to order some Little Neck clams and some vermouth cocktails for dinner, and a roast and some Brussels sprouts and the assemblings of a salad: and in it I am ingrainedly domestic, dreadfully useful, a strong pillar of the vast good nice world.

Afternoons I go out to a modiste's to fit a gown, or to a mild bridge-party along with other suitable women, or to a matinee with a suitable neighbor. Everything is perfectly right in my insides and in my thoughts: my thoughts run in little troughs in which there is no leakage or deviation, thoughts of a dreadful niceness, thoughts which ever presuppose potted plants on my window-sills.

Evenings I go out with my husband, or sit around with my husband, or take leave of him for a few hours at the hall door.

My husband would be the sort of man that is called a Good Scout. And he would have married me not for my wistfulness or wickedness or weirdness but for that I am a proper Shape and Size, with a smooth proper covering of flesh, to make a suitable sizable wife. And he would be a heavy grappling anchor to hold me fast in an ocean of domesticness.

Men of the genus Good Scout are all fiercely alike. All women, no matter what their genus, are exceptions to the rule. But men - rich men, poor men, beggar-men, thieves: so only they are Good Scouts - are of marvelous sameness. It comes from the want of minute lifelong pinpricking care of petticoats and potted plants - a detailed intensely personal sort of pain which touches dull solid tones of individuality with vivid various spots of color.

Men are made in "job lots" like their own cravats. Their cravats will differ in texture and color and quality and price. But each one is innately necktie. Use it as a garter or a tourniquet or a strangler's noose: it still is a man's deadly necktie. Its use may be ruined but its necktique is deathless. Except poets - and perhaps scientists - men are themselves like that. They cannot get away from the Adam. Nor can women get away from the Eve. But Eve was not a type but a somewhat pleasant human ensemble. While Adam was a type and a sufficiently nasty one: a rotter and a welcher: doubtless the Good Scout type of his day.

A Good Scout is the sort of man who if a woman trusts him with one one-hundredth of her heart will take the whole heart and twist and batter it: and read the paper and smoke his pipe and pay the bills: serenely unaware.

Which is beside the point in this. For in this image all my marriedness is a thing of outer Shape and Size and Suitableness. The odd but natural sequence is that I make an excellent wife. Excellent is the word. I keep a neat house with no dust left in the corners and no dead leaves on the potted plants. My husband is well looked after as to breakfasts and dinners and bodily comfort, and I am rigidly square with him and chastely true to him.

If, some dinnertime, as I sit opposite him in a soft pretty chiffon gown, my secret thoughts overflow their troughs and I passionately forget the potted plants and the window-sills and want horribly to rise up and bloodily murder my husband for being such a Good Scout: that would be a genuinely powerless matter, a cobweb trifle, compared with my actual potent Shape and Size which are so suitable for a wife.

I make truly and simply an excellent wife.

- *by God and my Soul-and-bones! it would be honester, finer, sweeter - more* comfortable *to be the dirty beggar-woman in the wet slippery streets -*

But it's facilely fancied because I am of Right Dimensions to be some Good Scout's wife.

A curious subtly pitfalled world: in it my Shape and Size, and my Weight which is also Right, could betray me into being an excellent wife: and by that a lying chattel, an inexpressibly damaged woman.

*

Ice-Water, Corrosive Acid, and Human Breath

To-morrow

I have love for two towns. One is this Butte that I tiredly love inside me. And the other is New York that I smoothly love with all my surfaces.

It is some years - a little lump of years - since I have seen New York: and it is two thousand miles away. So I see and feel its hard sweet lurid magnetism now ten times sharper than when I lived in it. But I felt it sudden and sharp at every turn then. A surface emotion which hits one's flesh and spreads wide over one's area is more exciting than a spirit emotion which pierces inward at one tiny point: an ice shower-bath on the white skin is more anguishing than an ice-water drink down the red throat. The spirit emotion lives longer and works more damage and buries itself at last in proud shaded soul-reserves. The surface-emotion stays always on the surface and lives actively in the front of one's senses and musings.

The feel of New York is a mixture of ice-water, a corrosive acid, and human breath sweeping someway warmish against one's flesh.

It is immensely ungentle, New York: immensely human: immensely intriguing to all one's selves. It is too big to have prejudices and traditions of locality: so it leaves its dwellers free, by ones and multitudes, to be human beings.

In South Bend and Toledo and Beloit and St. Paul and all the tight-built inland towns they murder you with narrowness and harshness and rancorous ill-will: they are scowlingly annoyed with you for making them murder you.

In New York they murder you with a large soft wave of indifferent insolence - no annoyance, no friction. New York eats you as it eats its dinner, rather liking you.

And my love for New York is made of liking: a made of liking: a plaisance of liking.

I like New York with a charmed restfulness for varied things in it: subways, and Fourth Avenue, and the River, and Fifth Avenue on a sunny October afternoon, and the statue of Nathan Hale, and old cockroachy downtown buildings, and the soft rich whelming creamy boiling-chocolate fragrance from the Huyler factory in Irving Place. And mostly I like it for the people in it - People - Persons - People: they are human beings.

In the inland towns people are half-afraid of thoughts, half-afraid of spoken words, half-afraid of each other, half afraid of the fact of being human.

In New York they are not afraid of any humanness. Even when they are in themselves craven-cowardly, cowardly enough to turn their own stomachs, they still turn their humanness unfearfully face-outward like upturned faces of a pack of cards.

An Italian organ-grinder grinding out his loud fierce music in a long deep New York side-street is a human organ-grinder: he bestows his rasped melody widely on everybody in ear-shot, not individually - since all around him is a spreading world of strangers - but jointly. So it feels-like.

A beggar-woman at a subway entrance with a whine and a dirty face and the deadly black cape and chicken-coopish beggar-odor is a human beggar-woman. She throws out an inner savor of herself like a soiled aura on all collectively who pass her. Each-and-all of New York by tolerating and owning her partakes of her mean human essence.

A stout-hearted worn-bodied Jew factory girl working at a hard greasy little machine day after day gives all New York her bit of young virtue which is hardy and heroic and unaware: the whole Island of looseness and vice has an equal gift of impregnable surprising sordid purity thriving on sixes and sevens of poor dollars-a-week.

All of it is because New York is one Large Condition made of human breaths and the worn scrapings of tired Youth rather than one large town made of individuals and stone houses.

And in that is an odd enchantment for me who am born and grown in the places of Half-fear with an old isolated whole fear always on me.

In New York I am a partaker of that smooth manna of humanness as I am of the air and the sunshine and the little black specks of coal-soot: partly from choice, partly willy-nilly, partly in the sweeping unanalyzable pell-mell-ness of massed human nature.

And it is in New York I have those strangest things of all: human friend-ships. Not many friendships and not of spent familiarities: for I don't like actual human beings too much around me. But yet friendships made of the edges of thoughts and vivid pathos and pregnant odds and ends of nervous human flesh and fire.

It is in New York I go to the apartment of a Friend at the end of an af-ternoon. In the apartment are some persons having tea, men and women. The Friend greets me at the door. She wears maybe a dress of thin dark and light silk, shaped in the quaint outlandish fashion of the hour. And she has shrewd kindly eyes like a Rembrandt portrait, and a worn New-York-ish Latin-ish brain and heart both of which are made of steel, sparkle, and the very plain red meat of living. She says, "Hello-Mary-Mac-Lane," and clasps my hand, and we exchange a glance of no real understanding at all but suggesting warmed challenge of personality, and an oblique sweet call of depth to depth, and of friendship which by mere force of preference and of our separate quality and *calibre* is true rather than false. So close and no closer may friendship be. And friendship, with-all, is closer than any love. It is the closest human beings ever come to meeting. In a New York doorway I, made in broad loneliness of self, get suddenly companion-warmed at the little pleasant twisted fire of someone else.

It might be so in some other town, even Beloit, but it feels only like New York to me.

I go in the room where the others are and they say, "Hello-Mary-Mac-Lane," and I drink some tea and listen and talk in fragments of half-meanings. And I get warmed and half-warmed and cooled and slightly scorched in the easeful unevenly-heated humanness of the women and men sitting around.

In the inland towns they throw their thoughts and ideas at you at tea-time, inland thoughts and ideas, which hit you and then drop off like little pebbles and nuts and hard green apples.

In New York they throw those things in the form of long ribbons, heated from being worn next their skin, which fly out and wrap around your skin: pleasantly or foolishly or fancifully.

The point of it is that nobody is afraid of that.

It is nothing fulfilling, nothing satisfying. It is merely human. It is half-lyric. It reassures me as a person: it makes me feel human in all my surfaces. Which are harder to humanize, in everybody, than any deepest deeps.

And it is therefore with all my surfaces, smoothly and restfully, I love New York.

*

Rhythm

To-morrow

Now and again I think I catch some truth by the sweat of its Rhythm.

Often I read the Beatitudes in the Sermon on the Mount and feel their truth in the blood-sweating tone of their Rhythm - Rhythm unspeakable and ecstatic.

The prophet Christ believed himself divine and was all Rhythm in his utterances: and so sounds true as the scheme of digestion and the laws of hygiene. He said, Blessed are they that mourn: for they shall be comforted.

Everybody who has tried it knows that to be true with the flawless Rhythmic truth of health and illness.

Mourn frightfully a day and the next day will be a day of soothed warmth and quiet like a grateful pitiful heat current in the breast. Mourn a week and that will come the week following. Mourn a year and the next year will be the year of peace. For anguish: peace. For peace: anguish. It never fails.

The great thing lacking in Christ, the sense of humor, permitted his perfect personal Rhythm. Humor oddly wants Rhythm. The human race is made in Rhythm like its beating heart: but humor is an "extra." Everybody is so full of lies that humor, an "extra," always wonderfully appetizing and out of season, and inexplicably God-given, feels like a great keystone of the race.

So it is: but in a lying race. And Christ in his beautiful dual role would lack humor. As a God come among the human race to save it, knowing it as he did: his measureless worldly wisdom being paramount even to his gentleness: his mind and his personal tenor could be set only in intense terrific gloom.

The Rhythm in the Beatitudes is equal Rhythm of sense and Rhythm of sound: Rhythm of music and Rhythm of meaning. Equally, half and half.

The most Rhythm thing in it is: Blessed are the pure in heart: for they shall see God.

I feel it soft-prickling just under my skin. Rhythm - Rhythm and ecstasy!

I have read it many times since I was a child: till I know it in my brain, in my Soul, in my hands, in my breast, in my throat, in my forehead, in my gray eyes, in my aching left foot. I know it and feel it by its Rhythm. There is barbarous justice in it. It cuts everybody off from seeing God.

Pure in heart I take to mean pure in motive. A fool has an equal chance with a philosopher: a harlot with a horse-thief: a nasty rag-picker with a small sweet child. But none is pure in motive.

Of other persons I don't judge. But me I know to be murderously un-pure of heart.

If I could open a window or unlock a door with only the simple mechanical motive in the act - But I can't. There's a romantic impurity in even the look of my hand as it touches the window-sash or the door-key. There's a pervasive delicate infusion of impure motive all over me, Soul and bones, as I perform the act. It is one curse in the Necklace which God himself bestowed on me so long ago.

It is not my fault that I am un-pure in heart.

And it is not God's. It is a comfort to me that I can reason out that it is not God's fault. He knew I needed the Necklace and each blue-green stone in it to rhyme and balance me. In the wide surprisingness of the universe everything will be rhymed and balanced. In me, being savagely complex, that balancing took a bit of doing: hence my unusual Necklace. It comforts me that I can reach that analytic point. It leaves me a lightning conviction that God is worth seeing.

And if a day dawns for me when I can open a door with no ulterior motive: thinking only of the door and the fine small muscular power of smooth hand and supple wrist given me to open it: thinking only that I want to get the door open: then back of that door I know I shall see God!

It is so written in that barbarous blood-sweating worldly Rhythm on the Mount.

*

A Prayer-Feeling

So it is finished: and I have oddly Failed.

I have slyly Succeeded and oddly Failed in equal degree.

I have Failed because I am too cowardly and too weak and too dishonest to write certain bruised and self-accusing places in my Soul and in my Heart and in my Mind which rightly come in the scope of this: there are the Stern and Delicate Voices one closes one's ears against: there are the starry grimy Actualities one drops from one's hands: there are the Thoughts one Does Not Think. Yet and yet: they too are in it, hanging cobweb-ish on my wordings and colons.

It is not a strong tale, and that is very well. This book is less I-written than it is I-myself. And Just Beneath The Skin no person is strong: not Theodore Roosevelt, true fearless American: not Bonaparte, splendid tyrant: not Joan of Arc, titanic martyr. They are strong in their depths and strong on the outside. So are many others. So am I, I think. But just under the skin all who are human are roundly weak.

Roundly weak, every one.

And with that, in my case, False.

This primarily is the picture of one who is made-False: False from her fingertips to her innermost concept.

It is belike because of that that this, as itself, oddly Fails.

It is as if I have made a portrait not of Me, but of a Room I have just quitted. My Gloves are left on a chair: my Hat is left on a couch: my taken-off Shoes are left on the floor: my faint-smelling Handkerchief is dropped by the door: my round ribboned Garter is hanging on the door-knob: my Breath is in the air: my Grief is on the walls clinging like smoke: my flat Despair is on the petunia-leaves in the window: my fragrant Horridness lingers in the curtains. I am not there! But I - *I have just Quitted that Room!* - Therein I have slyly Succeeded.

*

My feeling at my book's-end is a prayer-feeling, both frantic and quiet: God have mercy on me! but not unless you want to.

And I feel barbarous and utterly solitary, solitary from here to Jericho, solitary from here to the cool stars.

There comes off the grim gray east hills a soft whelming taste of Sunset, bloody and full of human marrows.

And I feel a need of great Pain or great Sin to make and break me, Soul and bones.

*

FURTHER READING

NOTES

Atherton, Gertrude. *Perch of the Devil*. Frederick A. Stokes, New York, 1914, pp 37, 173.

- - - - - - - . *Adventures of a Novelist*. Liveright, New York, 1932, pp 490-492.

Burlingame, Merrill K. and Toole, K.R. *A History of Montana*. Lewis Historical Publishing Co., New York, 1957, vol. II, p 286.

Brooks, Van Wyck. *The Confident Years*. Dutton, New York, 1952, pp 319-320, 469.

Brownlow, Kevin. *Behind the Mask of Innocence: Sex, Violence and Crime - Films of Social Conscience in the Silent Era*. Alfred A. Knopf, New York, 1990, pp 30-33, 514-515.

Canfield, Mary Cass. *Grotesques and Other Reflections*. Harper & Bros., New York, 1927, pp 48-60. (Essay on *I, Mary MacLane*. Orig. appeared as "Mary MacLane and the Apparent Agonies of Introspective Pathology," under the by-line "Peter Savage," in *Vanity Fair*, June 1917.)

Derleth, August. *Still Small Voice*. Appleton-Century, New York, 1940, pp 58-59. (Biography of MacLane's *New York World* interviewer, Zona Gale.)

Doran, George H. *Chronicles of Barrabas - 1884-1934*. Harcourt-Brace, New York, 1934, pp 29-30.

Faderman, Lillian. *Surpassing the Love of Men: Romantic Friendship and Love Between Women From the Renaissance to the Present*. William Morrow, New York, 1981, pp 299-300.

- - - - - - - . *Odd Girls and Twilight Lovers: A History of Lesbian Life in America*. Columbia University Press, New York, 1991, p 113.

Ferlinghetti, Lawrence and Peters, Nancy. *Literary San Francisco*. City Lights Books, San Francisco, 1980, p 92.

Foster, Jeannette Howard. *Sex Variant Women in Literature*. Vantage, New York, 1956. (Reprinted by Diana Press, Baltimore, 1975.)

Garland, Hamlin. *Companions on the Trail*. Macmillan, New York, 1931, p 147.

Hall, Dr. G. Stanley. *Adolescence: Its Psychology, and its Relations to Physiology, Anthropology, Sociology, Sex, Crime, Religion, and Education*. Appleton, New York, 1904, vol. I, p 559-560; vol. II, p 629.

Katz, Jonathan Ned. *Gay American History*. Meridian, New York, 1992. (Rev. ed.; orig. pub. Crowell, New York, 1976.)

Kittredge, William and Smith, Annick, eds. *The Last Best Place: A Montana Anthology*. University of Washington Press, Seattle, 1991. (Reprints passages from *I Await* and *I, Mary*.)

Kramer, Sidney. *A History of Stone & Kimball and Herbert S. Stone & Co*. University of Chicago Press, Chicago, 1940.

Mencken, H.L. "The Butte Bashkirtseff," in *Prejudices - first series*. Alfred A. Knopf, New York, 1919, pp 123-128.

Richards, Dell. *Lesbian Lists*. Alyson Publications, Boston, 1990.

Ross, Ishbell. *Ladies of the Press*. Harper, New York, 1936, p 419.

Rudnick, Lois Palken. *Mabel Dodge Luhan: New Woman, New Worlds*. University of New Mexico Press, Albuquerque, 1984, pp 139-140.

Spacks, Patricia Meyer. *The Female Imagination*. Alfred A. Knopf, New York, 1975, pp 6, 166, 171-180, 182, 184, 189, 192, 205, 218, 250, 316, 317.

Truitt, Evelyn M. *Who Was Who on Screen*. R.R. Bowker & Co., New York, 1977, p 293.

Workers of the Writers' Program of the WPA in the State of Montana. *Montana - A State Guide Book*. Viking Press, New York, 1939, p 103.

- - - - - - - . *Copper Camp: Stories of the World's Greatest Mining Town - Butte, Montana*. Hastings House, New York, 1943, pp 1, 257-258.

386. The identity of M- T- is unknown.

387. *devasted* - Old variant of "devastated."

388. *winged word* - Orig. an Homeric phrase, later taken up by Carlyle; sometimes poetically rendered "wing'd word."

391. *rowelling* - Mid. English: a wheel with sharp teeth inserted into a spur's shank-end.

392. *To-morrow and* - Spoken by Macbeth (v:5): *To-morrow, and to-morrow, and to-morrow, / Creeps in this petty pace from day to day, / To the last syllable of recorded time, / And all our yesterdays have lighted fools / The way to dusty death. Out, out, brief candle!*

395. *incalescent* - Growing intenser or hotter.

395. *pierce the* - Poss. ref. to stanza 33 of Shelley's poem "The Revolt of Islam" (pub. 1818): *But more he loathed and hated the clear light / Of wisdom and free thought, and more did fear, / Lest, kindled once, its beams might pierce the night, / Even where his Idol stood; for, far and near / Did many a heart in Europe leap to hear*; less likely, poss. ref. to anon. (prob. because near-treasonous) English poem "America, An Ode" (pub. 1776) 11:3: *Heaven her blazing portal spreads; / Shafts of glory pierce the night; / Lo! the bright van the royal patriot leads, / Founder of laws, and arbiter of right*

395. *stays* - Ref. to a corset.

396. *put to it* - Phrase used in law courts: a pointed issue to be heard or decided upon.

396. *lightning and* - From stanza 12 of Shelley's poem "Adonais, An Elegy on the Death of John Keats" (1821): *And pass into the panting heart beneath / With lightning and with music: the damp death / Quenched its caress upon his icy lips*

397. *sucking dove's* - From Shakespeare's *A Midsummer Night's Dream* 1:2 (spoken by Bottom): *But I will aggravate my voice so that I will roar you as gently as any sucking dove. I will roar you an 'twere any nightingale.*

399. *voile* - Fr.: "veil"; a lightweight, shear, soft cotton or cotton-blended fabric.

402. *hoyden* - Roisterous girl; orig. a rude youth; from Dutch *heiden*: heathen, boor.

402. *Nick Carter* - Dime-novel detective; first appeared in 1886 in *The Old Detective's Pupil; or, The Mysterious Crime of Madison Square* by John R. Coryell (story by Ormond G. Smith).

402. *Lady Audley's Secret* - Early true-crime-based novel (1862) by English novelist Mary Elizabeth Braddon (1837-1915); centers on socially-climbing bigamous female criminal; sensation in its time; features three secondary female chars. distinguished respectively by tomboyishness, social restraint, and loneliness.

402. *Lena Rivers* - Novel (1856) by prolific popular writer Mary Jane Holmes (1825-1907); centers on spunky orphan displaced to live with family members who don't know what to do with her; the grandmother is heavily oppressive of all concerned.

403. *demi-vierge* - Fr.: "half-virgin" - One who has been partway sexually active but not to the point of intercourse; also sometimes a young person whose thoughts are no longer chaste.

404. William Collier (born William Morenus, 1864-1944) - Light comedian noted for a natural, understated manner, said to have influenced Noel Coward; after long career in vaudeville, moved to motion pictures.

405. *prepollence* - Quality of being dominant, supererogatory.

406-407. *Dover* - Line spoken by Mr. Finching's grimly oracular aunt in Dickens' *Little Dorrit* (serial pub. 1855-1857); the line's enigmatic quality has been much commented-upon.

409. *inversions* - "Inversion" would have unambiguously suggested homosexuality, then called (and thought of as) "sexual inversion"; *cf.* also p 524: "a wanderer in fields of inverted fungi."

413. *pinchbeck* - Spurious, as replacement; M curtails the imaginary lovers' potency by indicating they, as counterfeits, won't be kept around for long.

413. *incumbrance* - Uncommon variant of "encumbrance."

413. *nepenthe* - Mythical drug of Ancient Greece: inducer of forgetfulness (of pain or sorrow esp.); attempted actual prep.s believed to have been opioid in nature.

415. *vamps* - Section of shoe's "upper" between the toes and the ankle-break.

416. *Rocker* - Suburb of Butte, about 3 miles west of town.

419. *song of myself* - Poss. ref. to Whitman's epic poem.

423. *Churchill's* - One of Broadway's great mid-town "lobster palaces"; famed for vast dining room (1200 seats, 300 waiters) and cabaret entertainment; owned by ex-NYPD

Capt. Jim Churchill (1863-1930); popular with Theatrical District people; *cf.* p 307.

424. *naif* - Variant of "naive."

424. *over-souls* - Prob. ref. to Emerson's neo-Platonic concept of a single transcendent soul of mankind.

425. François Villon (birth name uncertain, *c.* 1431-poss. 1460s) - French thief, itinerant, poet; at once thematic and formal innovator, writer about the lower classes, and includer of thieves' argot into poetry; *cf.* p 523.

426. *Glim* - A light-source, or light given by such.

426. *Chape* - A buckle's metal tongue or a scabbard's metal trim or tip.

426. *Plash* - A spatter or gentle splash.

426. *Whelk* - A sea snail, often but not always member of family *Buccinidae.*

426. *Mauger* - Despite, regardless.

426. *Frush* - To crush (or disintegrate) by battering; appears in Shakespeare's *Troilus and Cressida* v:6 (spoken by Hector): *I like thy armour well; / I'll frush it and unlock the rivets all, / But I'll be master of it: wilt thou not, / beast, abide?*

426. *Gnurl* - A grippable knob or other small protuberance; usually, one of a series of small grooves or ridges on a metal object's edge(s) or surface(s).

426. *Yare* - Quick, ready, nimble.

426. *Hyaline* - Any glasslike substance; has specific affine meanings in entomology, ichthyology, histopathology.

427. *Melody of* - Ref. to poem "Ode on a Grecian Urn" (1820) by John Keats, specifically its famous lines 11-14: *Heard melodies are sweet, but those unheard / Are sweeter; therefore, ye soft pipes, play on; / Not to the sensual ear, but, more endear'd, / Pipe to the spirit ditties of no tone*

427. Lillian Walker (1887-1975) - American vaudeville actress, moved to silent movies in 1911; extremely popular in 1910s.

427. *lorette* - Courtesan.

429-430. *simpler and finer* - These may be variations on one of Blake's "Proverbs of Hell": "Sooner murder an infant in its cradle than nurse unacted desires" (from *The Marriage of Heaven and Hell*, writ. *c*. 1789-*c*. 1793).

434. *woful* - Variant of "woeful."

435. *Oliver* - Boy's suit-style: featured short trousers and prominent buttons; was often paired with a string-tie.

435. *serge-Norfolk* - Single-breasted pleated jacket or suit including same, worn loosely and with belt or half-belt; in blue, a serge Norfolk suit was the predominant nurses' uniform in World War I.

436. *countrymen* - From Brutus' pulpit-speech in *Julius Caesar* III:2: *Be patient till the last. Romans, countrymen, and lovers! hear me for my cause, and be silent, that you may hear: believe me for mine honour, and have respect to mine honour, that you may believe: censure me in your wisdom, and awake your senses, that you may the better judge.*

436. *devil-fish* - Poss. *Mobula mobular*, also "giant devil ray"; species of eagle ray, family *Myliobatidae*, found in Mediterranean, less commonly in Atlantic.

437. *the whistling winds* - Poss. from Pope's trans. of Homer's *Iliad* (install. pub. 1715-1720) and (collab. Broome *&* Fenton) *Odyssey* (pub. 1726), in both of which the phrase recurs.

438. *cats* - Ref. to familiar phrase (origin unknown): "A cat may look at a king."
438. *from his ... wander in* - From FitzGerald's translation of *The Rubaiyat*; first quote omits a beginning poetic "What!"; second omits a beginning "Oh."

439. *wine must* - From Sonnet 6 of Elizabeth Barrett Browning's *Sonnets From the Portuguese* (written *c*. 1845-1846, pub. 1850): *And what I dream include thee, as the wine / Must taste of its own grapes. And when I sue / God for myself, He hears that name of thine, / And sees within my eyes the tears of two.*

443. *"Bill" Sikes* - Char. in Dickens' *Oliver Twist* (serial pub. 1837-1839); a vicious criminal and, in time, murderer.

443. *book and* - Indicates religious ceremony; orig., method of excommunication mentioned in Shakespeare's *King John* III:3 (spoken by the Bastard): *Bell, book, and candle, shall not drive me back / When gold and silver becks me to come on*; appears in Bk XXI, Chapt. I of Malory's *Le Morte d'Arthur* (pub. 1585): *I shall curse you with book and bell and candle.*

443. *sam shu* - Alt. "samshoo" or "samshu" - burningly intense Chinese liquor; distilled

from rice or sorghum.

443. *to St.* - Trad. English nursery rhyme.

444. William A. Muldoon (1852-1933) - Prominent physical culture advocate, sometime actor; undefeated in Greco-Roman wrestling in his time.

444. Bernarr MacFadden (1868-1955) - Prominent physical culture advocate; focused on nutrition and bodybuilding; wrote over 100 books, touted sexual intercourse for health and pleasure; publ. text misspells his name.

448. *back from* - Genesis 19:26 (King James).

448. *Oh, the* - Song quoted in Guy de Maupassant's short story "The Viaticum" (English trans. 1903).

450. *calefacient* - A substance that causes a sensation of warmth.

452. *pace* - Cf. n. 392 p 584.

453. *Goose* - The rhyme is "The Old Woman And The Pedlar."

453. St. Simeon Stylites (*c.* 390-459) - Known for living for 39 years on a small platform atop a pillar in Syria; subj. of eponymous poem by Tennyson (pub. 1842).

453. *Lanky Bob ... Carson* - Ref. to Corbett-Fitzsimmons boxing match at Carson City, Nevada (1894); British boxer Robert J. Fitzsimmons (1863-1917) wrested heavyweight title from Irish-American James J. Corbett (1866-1933) in a surprise win; subj. captured in a documentary film - at 100 minutes, the longest to that date; only fragments remain.

453. *Gal* - M misquotes title of song: "My Gal is a High-Born Lady" (1886), lyr. & mus. Barney Fagan.

454. *Dare-devil Dick* - 19th c. boys' adventure stories, sold in some printings for a penny per.

454. *Chautauqua* - Nationwide adult-educating movement of the time; featured touring groups of lecturers and entertainers; often performed in tents; "entertain and instruct" was a common phrase ref. to them.

454. *Widow* - Ref. to Champagne wine innovator Barbe-Nicole Cliquot *née* Ponsardin (1777-1866), widow (Fr. "veuve") of Philippe Clicquot-Muiron; the house her husband founded (and she controlled after his death) is Veuve Clicquot Ponsardin

458. *bone-brained* - A reminder that even highly individuated persons may remain in the offensive group-think of their time; while such refs. in M's work are rare (and are contradicted by other statements and her life-course), they do exist - *cf.* p 320 on race.

459. Inez Haynes Irwin (*née* Gillmore, 1873-1970) - Author, feminist, member of the National Women's Party.

460. *to read* - Ref. to "Ode to a Nightingale" (pub. 1820).

460. *Celeste Aïda* - Act I romanza in Verdi's *Aida* (sung by Radamès).

460. Sarah Blanche Sweet (1896-1986) - American actress; noted for independence and strength.

460. *Marchioness ... Brass* - Chars. in Dickens' *Old Curiosity Shop* (serial pub. 1840-1841); M's quote is incorrect; actual (Chapt. 36): *"Go further away from the leg of mutton, or you'll be picking it, I know," said Miss Sally. / The girl withdrew into a corner, while Miss Brass took a key from her pocket, and opening the safe, brought from it a dreary waste of cold potatoes, looking as eatable as Stonehenge.*

461. *this fellow* - From *Rip Van Winkle* (1859) by renowned American actor Joseph Jefferson (1829-1905); M's quote is incorrect; actual (Act IV, spoken by Derrick): *Here, give him a cold potato, and let him go.*

461. *baked* - From *Hamlet* I:2 (spoken by Hamlet): *Thrift, thrift, Horatio! the funeral baked meats / Did coldly furnish forth the marriage tables. / Would I had met my dearest foe in heaven / Or ever I had seen that day, Horatio!*

461. *Canterbury Pilgrims* - Presumably Chaucer's; a group of emigrants to New Zealand were known thus, but bore no substantive relationship to potatoes.

463. *Instead, through* - Ref. to 1 Corinthians 13:12: *For now we see through a glass, darkly; but then face to face: now I know in part; but then shall I know even as also I am known.* (King James)

463. *La Guzla* - 1827 hoax poetry-collection by Mérimée; passed off as translation from Serbo-Croatian; had a strong influence in Russia.

463. *Venus* - Ref. to "La Vénus d'Ille" (1837), a fantasy horror piece.

463. Geraldine Farrar (1882-1967) - Well-regarded American soprano and actress; upon her 1922 retirement and after, her large and passionately devoted following among

young women would be called "Gerry-flappers"; at least one writer has speculated on a homoerotic quality of the fan reaction; *cf.* Castle, Terry: *The Apparitional Lesbian: Female Homosexuality and Modern Culture*, Columbia Univ. Press, New York, 1995, Chapt. 9.

464. *sonant* - Having the quality of being voiced (as opposed to surd or asonant).

464. *Theda Bara* (born Theodosia Burr Goodman, 1885-1955) - One of the cinema's first sex symbols; the archetypal Vamp.

464. *maculate* - Contrary of "immaculate."

471. *shilling* - Slogan of Pall Mall cigarettes; straight-Turkish blend, marketed as a high-society item.

471. *Vantine* - Ref. to A.A. Vantine *& Co.*, a major exotics importer; "The Oriental Store"; had a large building at Fifth Ave. and Thirty-Ninth St. in Manhattan.

472. *an Eastman* - A slogan adopted by the Eastman Kodak Co. to combat the uncapitalized "Kodak"'s having become a generic term; M's "k" subverts the intent.

472. *Clarence Crane* - Innovative candy manufacturer from Cleveland, Ohio; invented Life Savers (1912); maintained a Chocolate Studio.

472. *Maillard* - American candy manufacturer; of high-class repute.

473. *octroi* - Authorities (orig., and generally, taxation authorities).

474. *world is* - Poss. from posth.-publ. (1694) *Journal of George Fox*; lived 1624-1691, founded Religious Society of Friends; phrase appears in journals several times.

476. *biograph* - Pop. term for a movie, derived from very early firm American Mutoscope *&* Biograph Company (parent co. founded 1895).

477. *Mist* - Apparent ref. to line in Virgil's *Aeneid* (1.462): *Sunt lacrimae rerum et mentem mortalia tangunt*; the translation M gives does not correspond to any found; however, as this was a standard (if difficult) assignment in Latin studies, M may be recalling her own.

478. *wavering* - Nine stone exactly would be 126 pounds.

480. *alphabetic ... 'drink all himself.'* - Untraceable ref. and quote; ed. speculates poss. ref. to Shlomo Yitzhaki (known as Rashi, 1040-1105), father of Talmudic and Tanakhic commentary, said (by Rabbi Zalman of Liadi) to have pressed "the wine of Torah";

the characters of the Hebrew alphabet in which his commentaries are printed are a special semi-cursive font.

482. *éclat* - Fr.: brilliant effect, result; connot. verges on flamboyant display.

482. *restfully* - Bans on absinthe had spread through Europe; by 1912 it was prohibited in the US.

486. *de-soie* - A fine or thin silk (or, later, rayon); can be to the point of gauziness.

487. Lord George Gordon (1751-1793), Pres. of the Protestant Association.

487. *riots* - London-convulsing uproar (1780) over 1778 Act that had partly loosened anti-Catholic laws; M's century is incorrect.

487. *Tyburn* - A Middlesex village known almost exclusively as the site of execution by hanging of London criminals (c. 1196-1783).

487. *illuminating* - An anachronism unless M means producing fake goods for the bookseller.

490. *being narrowly* - Likely an allusion to Euclid's fifth postulate.

491. *shockers ... dreadfuls* - Anachronisms; they emerged only in the 19th c.

492. *half-familiar ghosts* - An untraceable quotation.

493. *anchoretic* - In the manner of a self-denying religious recluse (*i.e.*, an anchorite).

493-494. *upon nothing* - From Mother Goose rhyme "A Strange Old Woman": *There was an old woman, and what do you think? / She lived upon nothing but victuals, and drink; / Victuals and drink were the chief of her diet, / And yet this old woman could never be quiet.*

495. *vestas* - Ref. to brand (Swan Vesta after 1906, orig. intro. 1883) of wax-soaked safety match with a shank of treated threads; its short length and damp-proof, wind-resistant qualities made it "the smoker's match"; in time, any waxed safety match was a "vesta" (*sans* capital), and some such appear in the Sherlock Holmes story "Silver Blaze" (1892); named for Roman goddess of home and hearth.

495. *petticoat* - From Mother Goose rhyme "Pussy-cat Mew": *Pussy-cat Mew jumped over a coal, / And in her best petticoat burnt a great hole. / Poor Pussy's weeping, she'll have no more milk / Until her best petticoat's mended with silk.*

496. Stanley Ketchel (1886-1910) - Widely-admired American middleweight, famed for fearlessness; would fight heavyweights, at times victoriously; got his start in a 1904 match in Butte.

496. Andrea del Sarto (1486-1530) - Florentine painter who straddled High Renaissance and very early Mannerist periods.   ˙

496. Boudica (?-*c.* 61) - Queen of the British Iaceniae, who uprose against Roman occupation; said to have been of Amazonian character.

496. Christopher Mathewson (1880-1925) - Prodigiously talented American pitcher; some of his statistics remain records (*e.g.* third-best all time wins, third-best shut-outs, eighth-best ERA).

496. *charlotte-russe* - Trad. holiday dessert of creamy consistency; made of eggs, whipping cream, and whiskey.

496. *lay in* - From Mother Goose rhyme "Robin and Richard": *Robin and Richard were two pretty men, / They lay in bed till the clock struck ten; / Then up starts Robin and looks at the sky, / "Oh, brother Richard, the sun's very high! / You go before, with the bottle and bag, / And I will come after on little Jack Nag ..."*

497. Jane Lee (1912-1957) - Scottish-born American child actress.

497. Amy Lawrence Lowell (1874-1925) - Distinguished New England poet, winner of posthumous Pulitzer Prize (1926).

498. *sleep* - From "Go to Sleep, My Dusky Baby" (1915), lyr. Frank Reader Rix (1853-1919), mus. Antonin Dvorak arr. Rix.

498. *tax* - Ref. to "Pierrot" (1882) by Guy de Maupassant (1850-1893).

498. *leaning* - Ref. to "The Blessed Damozel" (1st vers. pub. 1850) by Dante Gabriel Rossetti (1828-1882); written in Keats' manner - depicts a woman in Heaven looking down upon her lover on Earth and longing for reunion; it would mark Rossetti's career and be the subject of several of his paintings.

500. *unattuned* - Reason for quotation marks is unknown; the word was used at the time and before and not under proscription. A contemporaneous meaning seems to have been "in psychic or mental sympathy or connection"; *cf.* Beach, Rex: *The Ne'er-Do-Well* (ser. pub.), *Everybody's Magazine*, May 1911, p 678: *Promptly at seven o'clock on the following evening he returned to his post, and before he had been there five minutes*

knew that his presence was noticed. This was encouraging, so he focused his mental powers in an effort to communicate telepathically with the object of his desires. But she seemed unattuned, and coyly refrained from showing her face. He undertook to loiter gracefully, knowing himself to be the target of many eyes, but found it extremely hard to refrain from sitting on the curb - a manifestly unromantic attitude for a lovelorn swain.

501. *purling* - A river or stream's flowing swirlingly and with babbling sound

501. *mantling* - The hunching of a bird of prey over a kill to protect from competitors.

502. Valeska Suratt (1882-1962) - American actress and early Vamp (known as the screen's "Vampire Woman"); noted for the great hauteur of her garb.

502. *mænad* - A female disciple of Dionysus.

502. *Cyprian woman* - Euph. for prostitute; ultimately derived from an epithet for Venus ("the Cyprian goddess").

504. *gentleman's* - A general term for more refined games of chance (*e.g.* baccarat); here, poker is more likely meant.

505. *recherché* - Fr.: of refined, elegant appearance or manner; slight connot. of tending to the sumptuous.

506. *there an end* - Shakespearean phrase, *e.g. Macbeth* III:4, *Two Gentlemen of Verona* I:3.
515. *trainant* (properly "traînant") - Fr.: dragging, trawling; implicitly, disreputable.

515. *straight* - The term as a contrapositive to homosexuality would not be seen in print until *c.* 1941 (by 1868, however, it had appeared as a term for a chaste woman); the image-complex, however, is already present in M's thought: *direct repellent roads ... twisted ... straight ... straight-made* (pp 514-515).

517. *Timber* - Prominent mountain a few miles south of the city of Butte.

517. Fritz Augustus Heinze (1869-1914) - One of Butte's "Copper Kings"; ruthless competitor with Daly's Amalgamated Copper - bought judges, reduced miners' hours, ran as Anti-Monopoly Party candidate for Mayor; eventually was paid $12,000,000 by Amalgamated to leave Butte; moved to New York, where with his brothers had central role in causing the Panic of 1907, which became central argument for the Federal Reserve system.

518. *Noodle-ish and little* - Prob. ref. to small food and alcohol providers near Venus Alley behind Butte's famed Dumas Brothel on E. Mercury St. (*cf.* pp 293, 294, 300),

held to have been the country's longest-operated house of prostitution (1890-1982); prostitutes who had not made it into the Dumas or one of other houses received customers in cribs in the Alley which featured telephone lines to noodle parlors and bars for rapid deliveries.

519. *lid* - Ref. to statewide gambling prohibition, begun in 1910.

520. *Pickett's* - A futile charge against Union forces at Gettysburg (1863); though immensely costly in Southern casualties, considered by some the Confederacy's most-bravely fought; M refs. to battlefield valor to the point of death (*cf.* n. 520 p 594).

520. Arnold Winkelried (14th c., poss. legendary) - Swiss hero; charged into the pikes of Hapsburg Austrian troops at the Battle of Sempach (1386); his action, eventually fatal, opened the way for eventual Swiss victory; his name would come to be invoked for heroic bravery unto death in aid of a cause.

521. *Fetich* - Variant of "fetish."

522. *wefts* - From weaving: yarn drawn through the warps to form cloth.

522. François-Dominique Toussaint Louverture (1743-1803) - Leader of the Haitian Revolution; deported to France, where he died.

522. *pleasure* - From "The Realm of Fancy" (sometimes simply "Fancy") by Keats (pub. 1820).
523. - *outsoared* - From Shelley's "Adonais."

523. - *imagists* (usu. cap.) - Early-1910s group that coalesced around Ezra Pound, H.D., and Richard Aldington; favored compression and sharp-lined imagery; "Imagism" made its bow in Harriet Monroe's magazine *Poetry*, which Pound served as foreign correspondent (and to which M undoubtedly subscribed, likely from inception).

524. *deadlier* - From Kipling's poem "The Female of the Species" (pub. 1911) - *But the Woman that God gave him, every fibre of her frame / Proves her launched for one sole issue, armed and engined for the same; / And to serve that single issue, lest the generations fail, / The female of the species must be deadlier than the male.*

526. *uxoresque* - From Latin *uxor*: "wife"; still found in older English-language legal documents, sometimes abbrev. "ux."

527. *maggot ... nut* - "A maggot in a nut" is an old English expression; became prominent in 18th c.

527. *in-the-drawing* - Ref. to gambling: in the game, being in play.

529. *Hale* - Ref. to MacMonnies statue (1890); still stands in City Hall Park; *cf.* p 156.

530. *sixes and sevens* - Very old English phrase for chaos or disarray; connot. frazzledness.

533. *Jericho* - Poss. ref. to 2 Kings 2-4: *And Elijah said unto him, Elisha, tarry here, I pray thee; for the* LORD *hath sent me to Jericho. And he said, As the* LORD *liveth, and as thy soul liveth, I will not leave thee. So they came to Jericho.* (King James)

*

THIS
BOOK HAS
BEEN SET IN
ADOBE GARAMOND
PRO, A FONT BY ROBT.
SLIMBACH SPECIFICALLY
FOR DIGITAL TYPESETTING.
PERSONAL INSPECTION OF C.
GARAMOND'S ORIGINAL PUNCHES
INSPIRED A DESIGN FAITHFUL TO THE
ORIGINAL ROMAN TYPE, WHICH
TRADITIONALLY HAS BEEN
PAIRED WITH THE MORE
SLOPED, ENERGETIC
ITALICS CUT BY
R. GRANJON.

*

BOOK
DESIGN
HAS, IN YEARS
RECENT, DEPARTED
FROM CLASSICAL STRICTURES
AGAINST TYPOGRAPHICAL WIDOWS
AND ORPHANS. GIVEN THE NATURE
OF THIS TEXT, THE DECISION WAS
MADE TO HOLD RIGIDLY TO
PAGEBLOCK GEOMETRY
AND PERMIT WIDOWS
AND ORPHANS
FREELY.

*

* COMING NEXT *

Mary MacLane - a 19-year-old diarist from the early 20th century, still influential today - was the first of the modern media personalities. Now, her whole story is being told in a series of books from Petrarca Press.

On the heels of the successful launch of a 600-page anthology, *Human Days: A Mary MacLane Reader*, we are proud to announce 2015 release of two new books in our MacLane Series: *Mary in The Press: Miss MacLane & Her Fame* and the first-ever complete study of MacLane's life, career, and influence, *A Quite Unusual Intensity of Life: The Lives, Works, and Influence of Mary MacLane*.

Mary in The Press provides, for the first time, more than one thousand pages of interviews, news stories, reminiscences, attacks, opinions, plaudits, personal letters, cartoons, photographs, and more - almost all unseen for a century. With a detailed introduction and lengthy footnotes and bibliography, this mammoth two-volume edition unfolds for the first time the enormous controversy - and adoration - over the writer a forthcoming PBS documentary calls "The First Woman of the Twentieth Century."

A Quite Unusual Intensity of Life goes beyond the usual biography to unfold Mary MacLane's inner and outer worlds; the people she knew and loved; her influences, and her influence on the future; her life outside of writing as a gambler extraordinaire and silent film writer star; the inner secrets of her unique, still-compelling literary style - and much more.

Michael R. Brown, foremost MacLane scholar in the world today, says of these two books: "This is the other half of Mary's story, and it's taken decades of research to tell it. She gave herself totally in her writing, and the world's slowly remembering now. These are the books I wish I'd had at my side when I read those first words, thirty years ago."

Check http://marymaclane.com for exclusive content, updates, and all news about the ongoing discovery of Mary MacLane. For publication information and pre-ordering for *Mary in The Press* and *A Quite Unusual Intensity of Life*, email groupmail@petrarcapress.com or dial 530-566-6615. ISBN and SAN information forthcoming.

*

Adobe Garamond Pro * Body: 11.5 pts, lead: 12 pts. * Notes: 10 pts, lead: 11.175 pts. *
Page: 6in. x 9in. * Margins: top 1 in., bottom 1.375 in., inner 0.91 in., outer 0.7213 in.
Text width 4.3687 in. * Normal indent: 0.1667 in. * Fleuron from LTC Vine Leaves

www.ingramcontent.com/pod-product-compliance
Lightning Source LLC
Chambersburg PA
CBHW020614250626
47154CB00004B/1511